TOPSY

The Story of a Golden-Haired Chow

History of Ideas Series
Paul Roazen, Series Editor

TOPSY

The Story of a Golden-Haired Chow

Marie Bonaparte

With a new introduction by Gary Genosko

Transaction Publishers
New Brunswick (U.S.A.) and London (U.K.)

New material this edition copyright © 1994 by Transaction Publishers,
New Brunswick, New Jersey 08903
Originally published in 1940 by The Pushkin Press

Library of Congress Catalog Number: 93-26306
ISBN: 1–56000–127–5
Printed in the United States of America

Library of Congress Cataloging-in-Publication Data

Bonaparte, Marie, Princess, 1882-1962
    [Topsy, chow-chow au poil d'or. English]
    Topsy : the story of a golden-haired chow / Marie Bonaparte ; with
a new introduction by Gary Genosko.
        p.   cm. — (History of ideas series)
    Includes bibliographical references.
    ISBN 1-56000-127-5
    1. Bonaparte, Marie, Princess, 1882-1962. 2. Psychoanalysts—
Biography. 3. Chow chows (Dogs)—Biography. I. Genosko, Gary.
II. Title. III. Series: History of ideas series (New Brunswick, N.J.)
RC339.52.B65A4713   1994
150.19'52'092—dc20
    [B]   93-26306
                                                           CIP

Contents

PART II—TOPSY IS HEALED

Introduction to the Transaction Edition

Dogs are rife in the psychoanalytic bestiary. Anyone familiar with the biographical details of Sigmund Freud's life would acknowledge that he was a dog lover. Indeed, Freud's devotion to dogs is the stuff of psychoanalytic legend. Freud's dogs circulated among his other "precious things" (everything on display in his study) in the daily life of the household. It would be a mistake to separate the affectionate attention given to these animals in the emotional life of the family from Freud's analytic practice and theoretical work. Freud's biographers and analysands have, for instance, attested to the presence of his dog(s) during the analytic hour. In fact, any reader of Freud would have noticed that his work contains many animals, especially domesticated animals, which were not exclusively introduced by his patients. References to his and other dogs abound in Freud's letters, diary, theoretical texts (most importantly in his papers on technique and case histories), and work in translation. What significance can we afford to this canine element in Freud's life and work and, more generally, to its place in the psychoanalytic bestiary as a whole?

First and foremost, let's be clear about the dogs in question. This task is not as simple as it may first appear. Freud's first dog was a chow named Lun Yug. Acquired from Dorothy Burlingham in 1928, Lun Yug "unfortunately survived only fifteen months," according to Ernest Jones. Jones explains that in August 1929, after disappearing in the train station in Salzburg while being taken to Vienna by Eva Rosenfeld, Lun Yug was found dead on the tracks a few days later.[1] Before the arrival of Freud's most

1

famous chow Jofi (Lun Yug's sister) in March 1930, several references to a certain Adda appeared in Freud's diary in November 1929. Michael Molnar suggests that Adda may "have been an animal, perhaps a substitute dog,"[2] although in September 1930 Freud, according to Anna, was not yet prepared emotionally to acquire a new dog.

For a brief time, then, Berggasse 19 remained a one-dog household since Anna's Alsatian Wolf, acquired several years earlier (ca. 1925) to accompany her on solitary walks, remained on the scene. Anyone who has visited "Anna's room" in the Freud Museum at 20 Maresfield Gardens in London would have noticed the handsome black and white framed photograph (under which one finds a "poem") of Wolf hanging on the wall beside her loom, while a woven portrait of Jofi adorns the wall above her couch. The photograph was a birthday present from Anna to her father on the occasion of his seventieth birthday in 1926. Molnar explains that "the tradition of the dogs presenting a poem [to Freud] had begun in 1926 with a rhyme from Wolf."[3] Several examples of such doggerel are provided by Molnar, although he does not include this verse, which reads in translation:

> On account of the coming of much of the clan
> a house ban.
> Now 'gainst his normal demeanor and noise
> silently poised.
> His love for the friendly as edible
> as with sucked-up thermometers, immeasurable.
> Thus kept from the banquet so nourishing and fair
> he gets from the table scraps none of his share.
> Unwavering true: 'spite of fleeting pleasure's bite.
> He withdraws, quite dog-like.

Like a similar gift delivered to Freud by a tortoise on his birthday in 1930 while he was visiting his son Ernst in Berlin, the verse plays affectionately with familial incidents relating to disciplining the dog. While inquiries about the health of one's dog are common features of letters written home from afar—one need only read Marshall McLuhan's letters to his family in Canada from Cambridge in the mid-1930s to get a sense of how much he missed his dog Rags—such verse from a "child" to a parent but "signed" by a dog is certainly not unknown, and a good example may be found in Glenn Gould's doggerel valentine written at approximately seven years to his mother on the behalf of his Irish setter Nicky.[4] Since for Freud the relationship between dogs and children was strong, the dog was an ideal choice to deliver a childlike gift. The tortoise was delightful, but a "poor substitute" for Jofi, Freud remarked.[5]

Freud could be a reluctant disciplinarian. When in 1927 Wolf bit Ernest Jones, Freud explained in a letter to Max Eitingon, "I had to punish him for that, but did so very reluctantly, for he—Jones—deserved it."[6] Jones was no stranger to dog bites. In his autobiography *Free Associations*, Jones recalls a episode during his years in Toronto (1908–13) in which he was bit by a "savage dog" while defending his terrier.[7] Freud's reluctance to punish Wolf, however, followed from his view that dogs, unlike people, display no ambivalence in their object relations: "Dogs love their friends and bite their enemies." Although Freud was not aware of Jones's phobic reaction to wolves, and especially to wolflike dogs such as Alsatians, his view of canine love and hate behaviors impressed Jones. Jones wrote in his autobiography, "On my first meeting . . . with Anna Freud's Alsatian, who was unfortunately called 'Wolf,' my fears were confirmed. He flew at me and tore a piece of my thigh. Freud, who was present, sagely remarked on how dogs instinctively recognise those who dislike them or are afraid of them, and at once treat them as enemies."[8] For his part, Jones seemed unaware that Freud thought he deserved it!

Wolf spent some ten years with the Freud family (ca. 1925–36). Freud came to refer to him as "an old gentleman," since the dog was close to his own age in dog years. Freud's paternal fondness for Anna's dog may have been strong enough to mask the sociosemiotic significance of the presence of an Alsatian (called a German shepherd), a breed which makes an ideal police dog, in a household idenitifed as Jewish. The very breed of dog acquired to protect Anna would come to be one of the many visible vehicles of the persecution of Jewish citizens in Austria and elsewhere. By the late 1930s, there was nothing ambivalent about German shepherds understood as cultural signs aligned with Nazism. Moreover, these dogs clearly did not choose their enemies. They were selectively bred, as Arnold Arluke and Boria Sax explain in their investigation of the contradictions of Nazi animal protection laws, "to represent and embody the spirit of National Socialism. Van Stephanitz, the creator of this breed, sought national status for a local population of coyote-like dogs in the 1920s that were to be regarded as racially better dogs, analogous to better bred humans"[9] The name of Anna's dog was descriptive; a German shepherd is a *Wolfehunde*. As well as Wolf's resemblance to a domesticated wolf, its name alone would have conjured National Socialist wolf imagery.[10]

Freud's affection for Wolf masked his projection onto dogs of freedom of choice and an uncomplicated natural state devoid of ambivalence, neither of which took into account his own insights into the processes of domestication, nor revealed much sensitivity to the effects of obedience training—a dominant theme in Anna's dog poems—and the dog's reliance upon its master/ mistress for food, comfort, and communication.

Jones was undoubtedly correct in pointing out that Freud's interest in canine ways was "evidently a sublimation of his very great fondness for young children which could no longer be gratified."[11] For Freud, the loss of a dog was akin in quality but not intensity to the loss of a child. Freud was always careful to qualify the relationship between dogs and children; for example, in 1927 he wrote to Jeanne Lampl-de Groot to the effect that "Wolf . . . has almost replaced the lost Heinerle" (Freud's grand-son Heinele Halberstadt, son of Freud's daughter Sophie, died in 1923 at four years, that is, three years after his mother passed away).[12]

While Freud found that dogs were more "attractive" than complicated adults, they were not in any straightforward way substitutes for children. Yet, since Wolf lived with the Freud family far longer than any other of their succession of dogs, including Jofi, and given that he outlived several persons for whom Freud felt dearly, it is evident that Wolf played an important role in Freud's domesticated, discontented civilization. Wolf was a longtime companion with whom Freud could momentarily retreat from the complexities of adulthood, reenchanting something of what he once described as the strong pre-phobic bond which united children and animals. Wolf, in short, solaced Freud. In turn, he could spoil Wolf, since this dog was a grandchild of sorts, whom he would not discipline in the manner of a parent.

Over the course of Jofi's life with Freud from March 1930 to January 1937, references to her occur frequently in his diary, letters, and family memorabilia (family snapshots and home movies often included the dog[s]), and touch upon a wide variety of everyday concerns familiar to any dog owner. In October 1931, Jofi's puppy Tattoun (a chow named Tatoun belonged to the Bonapartes) died of what may have been canine distemper. He had been with Freud for only nine months.[13] In April 1933, one of the pups of a second litter was also named Tattoun; another was named Fo after Freud's stone Dog of Fo.[14] Bonaparte's Tatoun lived until 1939.

Freud had, however, made other plans on the occasions of both of Jofi's pregnancies. Hilda Doolittle's (H.D.) companion Bryher (Winnifred Ellerman), whose pet name, incidentally, was Fido, not only paid for H.D.'s analysis with Freud but had contributed financially to the *Psychoanalytic Review* through Ernst Freud. At the time of the first litter, Freud had no means of repaying Bryher's kindness, but one. As Barbara Guest explains, Freud "offered Bryher one of the expected Jo-Fi puppies."[15] Recall that Tattoun—the only survivor of the first litter—lived a short life. Still, Bryher was in no position to accept Freud's offer since she already had several dogs and monkeys, and wrote to Freud expressing her regret. As the story goes, "the dénouement was that, after giving birth, Jo-Fi ate part of the [second] litter, and the one designated for Bryher bit someone and came to an early demise."[16]

It was with the name Tattoun that the canine concerns of

Freud and Marie Bonaparte began to overlap. Freud's two Tattouns were named after one of the dogs Bonaparte and her husband had acquired on behalf of their daughter Eugénie (in the fall of 1928), whose long struggle with pulmonary tuberculosis and a tubercular cyst on her leg stretched over several years. The loss of one of these dogs in 1929 brought a letter of condolence from Freud.[17] Eugénie's successful request for two canine companions broke her mother's ban on dogs upon which she had insisted up to this point on the grounds of her own painful loss of a fox terrier as a young girl. Although Tatoun ostensibly belonged to Prince George, the dog record is unclear since Eugénie seems to have had an Old English sheep dog as well as two unidentitifed little white dogs, in addition to the chow Tatoun. During the eary 1930s, a mate for Tatoun, Cheekee, was acquired. Their puppy Teaupi or Topsy, Princess Marie's dog, entered the psychoanalytic bestiary in 1935 when, after a winter heavy with obligations, travel, and an extended Easter vacation at her property in St. Tropez, Bonaparte returned to Paris and was advised that a lump had been discovered in Topsy's lip.[18] The diagnosis of a lymphosarcoma led Bonaparte to take Topsy to the Curie Institute for regular x-ray treatments. Bonaparte's *Topsy* was written between March 1935 and June 1936.[19]

Before we develop further the Freud-Bonaparte relationship, a few critical reflections on the place of dogs in Freud's practice are in order. One can only imagine the sort of atmosphere into which an analysand entered upon arriving for a session with Freud. In a room, then, that smelt of dogs and cigars, one would have had to contend with a rhythmical panting issuing from a sentient fixture at the foot of the couch. One might accuse Peter Gay of tidying up Freud's precious things when he notes that "the dog would sit quietly at the foot of the couch during the analytic hour."[20] Anna Freud also confirms the presence of the dog as the general rule: "Yo-Fie . . . patiently participated in all analytic hours."[21] H.D., however, attests to Jofi's presence with a mild reproach: "I was annoyed at the end of my session as Yofi would wander about and I felt that the Professor was more interested in Yofi than he was in my story."[22] The presence of his top dog did not trouble Freud in the least.

Doolittle describes in some detail how Jofi greeted her at the door: "A little lion-like creature came padding toward me—a lioness, as it happened. She had emerged from the inner sanctum or manifested from under or behind the couch . . . I bend down to greet this creature. But the Professor says, 'Do not touch her—she snaps—she is very difficult with strangers' . . . I am ready to take the risk . . . . I not only continue my gesture toward the little chow, but crouch on the floor so that she can snap better if she wants to. Yofi . . . snuggles her nose into my hand."[23] Feminist scholars such as Rachel Blau Duplessis have maintained that the domesticity of this scene veils Doolittle's nonverbal challenge to male gender authority.[24] In this case, domestic and analytic practices overlapped and facilitated the circulation of Jofi, even though Freud says nothing about the presence of a dog during analysis. In addition, one needs to keep in mind that H.D.'s pet name was Cat; that is, this Cat would not be intimidated by Freud's dog. In a room whose only professional touch, as Doolittle noted, was "the 'white napkin for the head,'" one cannot insist too much upon clinical neutrality and abstract professionalism. Freud's study was already a living museum, far richer and nuanced than what remains in virtue of the institutional housekeeping of the Freud museums in Vienna and London.

Neither Freud nor Doolittle were alone in this drifting dogbody. During a conversation with Kurt Eissler, Janet Malcolm noticed that "the room of Eissler's consultation room suddenly opened and a large dog walked in. He came over and sniffed me in a friendly but unintrusive way, and then trotted over to the analytic couch, jumped up on it, pawed at the blanket that lay folded at the foot until it looked like an unmade bed, and lay down and went to sleep."[25] What role does this *chienlit* play in the work of analysis? Has Eissler adopted one of Freud's affectations for good reason?

Freud's consulting room, like his manner, was his alone. His devotion to Jofi was so strong that he did not entertain the idea of sparing an analysand a confrontation with his dog; if we are to believe Ruth Mack Brunswick, the Wolf-Man could not avoid encountering Wolf during his visits with Freud in the years following his initial analysis.[26] The presence of Jofi was a wild card in the analytic session. Doolittle sums up the matter nicely: "I think that if the chow hadn't liked me, I would have left."[27]

A decade before the Freud family acquired its first dog, one finds in a paper on technique entitled "Observations On Transference-Love: Further Recommendations On The Technique of Psychoanalysis" (1915), a remarkable canine analogy adapted by Freud so as to reflect its origin in myth and to deliver a pointed message about transference. Freud's dogs circulated both textually and extratextually.

Freud insists in this paper that the analyst must not go to the dogs by way of the transference. His point is that transference-love is "induced" by the analytic treatment and "intensified" by resistance. This should come as no surprise to the physician, Freud thinks, and 'he' must not give the female analysand his love, that is, 'he' must not jeopardize the analysis by allowing himself to be seduced for the "sake of a fine experience." Freud writes:

> For the doctor, ethical motives unite with technical ones to restrain him from giving the patient his love. The aim he has to keep in view is that this woman, whose capacity for love is impaired by infantile fixations, should gain free command over a function which is of such inestimable importance to her; that she should not, however, dissipate it in the treatment, but keep it ready for the time when, after her treatment, the demands of real life make themselves felt. He must not stage the scene of a dog-race in which the prize was to be a garland of sausages (*ein Kranz von Würsten*) but which some humorist spoilt by throwing a single sausage on to the track. The result was, of course, that the dogs threw themselves upon it and forgot all about the race and the garland that was luring them to victory in the far distance.[28]

For Freud, the analyst should resemble a cold and remote dog star rather than a dog in heat; the latter approximates his view of an analysand subject to an intense transference. Both the analyst and the analysand must resist the opportunistic manoeuvres of the resistance which, like its analogical equivalent, the humorist, may intervene disadvantageously and, as it were, threaten the outcome of the treatment by making use of the transference-love for the sake of a single sausage or, if you like, for fleeting sexual satisfaction. In "loosening" the transference, the analyst must not be brought down to the level of a lover. The resistance is an *agent provocateur*, Freud writes, and it is poised to interrupt the difficult journey the analysand must undertake from illness to "real life" by leaving "her" grasping at sausages along the way. As soon as the analyst forgets the rules of technique, he fritters away the possibility of restoring the analysand's capacity for love in the long term.

Freud's dog race is no shaggy dog story. Although the manner in which he presents it does little to betray its origin, thereby testifying to his literary skills, the complex analogy appears to be a degenerate version of the Greek legend of Atalanta and the Golden Apples.[29] The legend is that Atalanta, the brave huntress who slew the boar on the Calydonian hunt, declared that she would marry the suitor who defeated her in a foot race. After many men had failed and paid the penalty of failure, which was death, a beautiful youth came forward to challenge her, after having witnessed the defeat of still another pretender. Before the race, this youth named Hippomenes beseeched Aphrodite for assistance, and she responded by providing him with three golden apples. At crucial moments during the race, he was to drop the apples one by one so as to distract and delay Atalanta. And so in this manner Hippomenes won the race.

The analogy is largely consistent from the legend to Freud's story of the dog race to its application to the technical and ethical issues raised by transference-love. Consider the following summary:

Apples, Sausages and Analysis

Figures	Sex	Event	Goal	Intervening Agent	Purpose*
Atalanta	f				distract
		race	marriage	Aphrodite/apples	Atalanta
Hippomenes	m				
dog	(f)				distract both
		race	ring of sausages	humorist/sausage	for a small reward
dog	(m)				
analysand	f				distract both
		analysis	cure†	resistance/transference	for fleeting pleasure
analyst	m				

* The purpose of the intervention is to distract one or both parties by means of a lure.

† The demand of "real life" towards which in practice the analysis moves is the future marriage of the female analysand. This is the goal of the analysis, which is, in this sense, a kind of psychical normalization for the so-called "institution of love". The resistance is an *agent provocateur,* a masculine force (*provocatrice* is rare in French).

The analyst must not stage the treatment as if it were a dog race of the sort described by Freud. Freud's remarks are directed at "younger men" since they are most likely to be led astray (as opposed to taking the lead), given the powerful emotional and physical rewards promised by the resistance. This is especially the case if these "men" have not yet experienced such rewards in the course of their lives. The analyst possesses a certain animal magnetism which requires him to reflect upon the intervening agencies which could derail the course of analysis.

When Freud considered the complications of transference-love, he chose a dog story, and he did so long before he acquired a dog and Jofi took her place at the foot of the couch. It is not difficult to imagine that a dog which rambled around the consulting room, after having served as a Cerberus-like gatekeeper, would complicate the transference by giving the resistance a ready excuse for a variety of evasive manoeuvres. By the same token, even the most well-behaved dog would respond to its master's cues, sub-threshold or otherwise (cooing, clicking, little terms of endearment, a gesture, etc), as well as other noises in the apartment. Freud's "evenly suspended attention" (*gleich-schwebende Aufmerksamkeit*)[30] would have had a beloved object at hand upon which to alight. As he bent his unconscious "like a receptive organ" to receive what the analysand had brought to consciousness from his or her own unconscious, the dog was always there, in the communicational channel. There is nothing neutral about the presence of a dog; puppy love puts one's attention off balance. In the end, one can only speculate on the effects of the presence of any dog during an analysis and question after how a pet fits into the management of the hour. Martin Freud offers us a clue by noting that his father often kept track of the length of the session by paying attention to Jofi's stirring which, as regular as clockwork, occurred at the end of the hour.[31] This was precisely what upset H.D. Of equal importance is the recognition that the domestic economy of the Freud household and the arrangement of his precious things played a significant and complex role in psychoanalytic practice and theory.

On January 11, 1937 Jofi was admitted to the hospital for surgery to remove two ovarian cysts. Although the operation was thought to have been a success, Jofi died suddenly of heart failure on January 14. "One cannot easily get over 7 years of intimacy," Freud confessed to Arnold Zweig.[32] The following day (January 15), Freud reacquired the chow Lün from Dorothy Burlingham. Unlike the lengthy period of mourning which followed the loss of Lun-Yug, Freud "could not get on without a dog," as Jones put it, at this advanced stage of his life.[33] Lün originally belonged to Freud and had to be given away—first to the Deutschs who later transferred her to the Burlinghams—because Jofi could not tolerate a rival. The familiar Lün helped assuage Freud's pain over the loss of Jofi. Less lion-like in appearance than Jofi, Lün was nonetheless intelligent, pretty and more tender than Jofi, in Freud's estimation.[34] The return of Lün coincided with the return of another precious thing: Freud's correspondence with Wilhelm Fliess, delivered by Princess Marie, a fellow dog lover.

Jones recounts the events of an episode concerning Lün related by Felix Deutsch. When Deutsch took charge of Lün for Burlingham while she was on vacation, he exclaimed that "This dog is a psychosomatic case, indeed!" His job as dog-sitter was to provide an "anti-baby-sitting" service since Lün's life would be threatened if she were to be impregnated, owing to the narrowness of her pelvis. Despite Deutsch's best intentions, she began to display "the unmistakable signs of pregnancy" after a visit with the neighbour's "beautiful male poodle." Deutsch continues:

> Nothing could be done at the moment more than wait and see. Several weeks went by without any change in her behavior. At the end of the second month, however, the teats began to swell and colastrum appeared. She began to get fat rapidly. When on the street, she scratched and dug holes in the ground, altogether unmistakable signs of pregnancy. I resigned myself to the inevitable, but nothing happened.
>
> On the contrary, in the fourth month, instead of increasing, these signs started to decrease. I rushed with the dog to the veterinarian. Diagnosis: pseudocyesis. Have you ever heard of a dog with a false pregnancy? I am almost inclined to say: 'That can only happen to the dog of an analyst!'[35]

Pseudocyesis or false pregnancy is a normal phenomenon in dogs, as is its spontaneous remission. Deutsch's inclination to ironically ascribe the psychological origin of the false pregnancy to its owner-analyst led Jones to remark: "Freud also must have been amused at this example of the power of wish-fulfillment combined with the phenomenon of somatic compliancy."[36] The emotional context of this episode is complex. Freud had a genuine sense that he and his dogs shared an intimate mutual understanding, a belonging together free of ambivalence, understood by

Jones in terms of Freud's sublimation of his love for children. The physical and psychological signs characteristic of pregnancy displayed by Lün not only stand on the whole as an exemplary instance of psychosomatic compliance with respect to a mother instinct but, as Jones and Deutsch suggest, need to be understood in relation to Freud's fondness for his dog's and the latter's ability to respond to the needs of their owner or handler. A false pregnancy is often 'treated' because of the psychological effects it has on the dog's owner. This self-recognition may have been what amused both Deutsch and Freud.

Bonaparte's *Topsy, chow chow au poil d'or* was published in 1937. The completed manuscript had been in the Freuds' possession since December 1936, at which time Freud acknowledged its receipt in a letter to Bonaparte: "Just received your card from Athens and your manscript of the Topsy book. I love it; it is so movingly genuine and true. It is not an analytic work, of course, but the analyst's thirst for truth and knowledge can be perceived behind this production, too."[37] On April 9, 1938 Freud noted in his diary "Topsy translation finished,"[38] a task Anna had begun from a draft manscript some eighteen months earlier according to Jones.[39] Jones commented that "Freud entered fully into the spirit of the book—a fondness for chows was one of the many links between him and the author—and liked it greatly."[40] The German translation by Anna and Sigmund, *Topsy, der goldhaarige Chow*, appeared in 1939; Princess Eugénie's English translation, *Topsy, The Story of a Golden-Haired Chow*, was published in 1940.[41]

In her foreword to a new German edition of *Topsy* republished in 1981, Anna evoked the circumstances in which her father worked: with the Nazi invasion of Austria (March 1938), the climate of apprehension had turned to fear, and Freud found himself without any analysands, house-bound (ultimately put under house arrest), lonely, ill, and uncertain about his family's future. It was in this state that he took up "an old occupation, the work of translation," in order to "do a favor in gratitude for her [Bonaparte's] unflagging helpfulness."[42] Anna is silent on her own role in the translation, adding that "it was not only the person of the author but, above all, the topic of the book which influenced Freud's choice." This favor also in a manner of speaking "repaid" Freud's own dogs, Anna wrote, for their years of companionship. Her father, Anna explained, turned away from the violent and destructive world of his fellow men to that of animals; a turn, then, toward a relationship full of affection, simplicity, and beauty. Ultimately, with the assistance of Bonaparte, the Freuds left Vienna on June 4, 1938, en route to London via Paris.

Both Celia Bertin and Molnar consider the story of Topsy to have been a means by which Freud could "distract" himself from the deteriorating political situation and the strain of waiting for the family's exit visas. In a study of *Topsy*, Lynn Whisnant Reiser maintains that "the persistent misplaced emphasis on the 'dog story' obscures the more profound issues" which may be seen in the parallels between the illnesses of Topsy, Freud, and Bonaparte's father;[43] for his part, Molnar believes that neither Anna nor Sigmund overlooked such parallels. In spite of Reiser's insistence, we have already seen numerous examples of how a succession of textual and extratextual dogs have influenced Freud's life and work. Moreover, this favor for Bonaparte and his own dogs was not an unusual way for Freud to repay someone, if one recalls how he sought to repay Bryher.

The so-called "dog story" does not, as Reiser suggests, limit one's critical appreciation of the psychoanalytic bestiary. On the contrary, dog stories are polysemous discourses which transcend their anecdotal status and open onto questions concerning technical, ethical, theoretical, emotional, and literary concerns around how psychoanalysis treats animals. Dogs may be counted among a variety of domesticated animals which influenced Freud's zoological vision. More generally, anthologies of dog stories have periodcally marked the literary landscapes of the nineteenth and twentieth centuries. To call Freud a dog lover and *Topsy* a dog story is to bring both into contact with a subgenre of fiction writing. The very idea of a "dog lover"—an idea as suggestive connotatively and nuanced psychosexually as 'petting'—may be apocryphal, as Jeanne Schinto suggests, but nonetheless raise the eyebrow of any psychoanalytic bestiarist attuned to literary expressions of zoophilia.[44]

In Freud's investigation of phobic animals in *Totem and Taboo*,[45] we are confronted with a pillar of the Freudian bestiary, as least as far as domesticated animals and male children are concerned. In children's animal phobias, animals are substitutes for the father. Phobic reactions to animals arise out of the Oedipus complex and Freud thought they were among the earliest of childhood psychoneuroses. Although a child may find some measure of relief from his ambivalent attitude toward his father by displacing this mixed emotion onto an animal, this displacement does not, of course, bring an end to the conflict, since the animal in question is regarded with both fear and interest.

Freud enlisted Sandor Ferenczi's case of Little Arpad to further his project of Oedipalizing totemism.[46] Arpad identitifed ambivalently with his totem animal: chickens or more generally poultry (domesticated fowl). Ferenczi's "Little Chanticleer" played with toy fowls by slaughtering and caressing them. Freud also described how his young patient Little Hans trotted around the household, neighing, while wearing a nose bag; Hans also bit his father and behaved in a fearless way towards him.[47] Little Arpad and Little Hans were both trapped in Freud's bestiary by the single apologue under which their phobias were subsumed. The cases assisted Freud in his effort to find the dead father behind the animal totem in totemic practices, and to find the substitution of the animal for the father in animal phobias. An ambivalent attitude toward the two principle taboos of totemism, which are also the primal wishes of children and the two crimes of Oedipus, is shared by "primitive savages" and children.

Freud also called the Wolf-Man's wolf a "totemic father-surrogate."[48] This patient had a conscious fear of wolves and an unconscious fear of his father; secondly, a further phase in his relationship with his father was expressed through the Wolf-Man's identification with Christ, loving son of his Father, the divine Father; the latter, Freud argued, was a surrogate father whom arrived on the scene sometime after animal totems had been eclipsed. Animal phobias and totemism are parallel products of phylo- and ontogenetic complexes: there is a phaseal development of the surrogate's form on the phylogenetic level (primal father—animal totem—human, male figure [Christ]); on the ontogenetic level, Freud found similar phases in the unfolding of the Wolf-Man's relationship with his father.

Freud displayed little interest in strong pre-phobic relations between children and animals, and he was not concerned with the positive relations which may be reestablished between them after a "successful" Oedipalization. His zoological vision was blinkered by his approach to animals as phobic objects, as sign vehicles for the siphoning of ambivalent affect, even though in his own relationships with dogs there were no traces of ambivalence, except at the end of his life at which time Lün would avoid him owing to the odor of the cancerous ulcer on his cheek.[49] During the period that Lün was in the quarantine pound at Ladbroke Gardens, London, a Pekinese named Jumbo was acquired as a replacement for the chow. This dog, however, became attached to the Freud's housemaid, Paula Fichtl, "the provider of nourishment."[50]

Freud's zoological vision was diminished by a second pillar of his psychoanalytic bestiary. As an urbanite, Freud's contact with animals was largely limited to the domesticated creatures of Viennese society: horses, dogs, cats, pigeons, and other birds, including the animals of the medical establishment. He undoubtedly had some contact with farm animals, if only from afar, and may even have glimpsed wild animals during his sporting walks in the Hohe Tauern; whether Freud visited the zoo at Schönbrunn on the outskirts of Vienna is unclear, although Little Hans had conducted some of his sexual researches there. Still, Hans was a town boy who had a town animal phobia. In addition to his field work at the zoo, Hans familiarized himself with giraffes and elephants by posting pictures of them on the wall above his bed. Animal phobias, Freud recognized, were largely contextual. If an animal phobia occurs as a sudden tear in hitherto intimate and equal relations between a child and certain animals, what is torn asunder is a relation of contiguity (close proximity such as that enjoyed by Hans with respect to the horses arriving at the loading dock across the street from where he lived). In certain circumstances, Freud conceded, the choice of a phobic animal may be determined by fairy tales and picturebooks (textual sources).

As a dog-loving urbanite, Freud was predisposed toward domesticated creatures. When it came to thinking animals in the case of the Wolf-Man, this disposition worked itself out accordingly. In this case Freud intially favoured an explanation which emphasized the textuality of the Wolf-Man's phobic animals (wolves) since they were "not . . . easily accessible to observation (such as a horse or a dog), but [were] known to him only from stories and picture books."[51] Although Freud at first bracketed horses and dogs, his ultimate choice of a model domesticate upon which to base his interpretation served notice of his own resistance to this "foreign" patient, and illustrated the theoretical power which dogs possessed for him. These dogs jumped their brackets and he maintained that the "wolves of the dream were actually sheep dogs."[52] As a child, the patient must have observed a pair of sheep dogs copulating *a tergo*, according to their nature, and displaced this sight onto his parents. If the Wolf-Man had not witnessed animal coitus, he nevertheless would have possessed the phylogenetic experience of having observed parental intercourse. Freud resisted giving a contextual basis to wolves. It did not occur to him that a Russian might dream of white wolves because such animals were found where he lived on his father's second estate in White Russia, in what was known as wolf-country.[53] Freud was already predisposed toward dogs before he acquired his first chow. Where wolves were, one might say, dogs shall be.

Many of the parallels between the illnesses of Topsy and Freud have been documented by Reiser, although this does not obviate the need for a close rereading of *Topsy*. Both suffered from tumors on the right side of the oral cavity which made chewing difficult; both were treated by palliative surgery, Roentgen rays and radium. Although Bonaparte did not mention Freud's cancer in Topsy, "she declared that the memory she was haunted by was that of her father, who had died of metastatic cancer of the prostate twelve years earlier."[54] Bonaparte's daughter Eugénie had suffered from a tubercular cyst in her right thigh and had undergone x-ray treatments. Topsy was both a charm against illness as much as a sign of it. But the fact that Topsy won her battle against cancer (unlike her mother Chiki who also died of cancer) and in turn nursed Bonaparte through her own illness "must have expressed," Reiser thinks, "both for Marie Bonaparte and for the Freuds, the wish that Freud . . . would yet recover."[55] Reiser suggests that the focus on Topsy gave both the Freuds and Bonaparte a way "to acknowledge the nature of their suffering, and yet to keep some distance."[56] For as intimate as Freud and Bonaparte were, Anna remained her father's guardian.

Topsy consists of two parts. The first "Topsy Is Ill," and the second "Topsy Is Healed." The "Prologue—In Dogland" introduces the reader to the canine history of the Bonaparte household. Bonaparte describes Tatoun and Topsy (father and daughter)—the last surviving dogs of the original menagerie—as "two canine lares," suggesting cherished possessions and guardian spirits.[57] These "little lions" flanked the doorway and the Princess brushed past them as if passing through a hair-lined opening. It was Bonaparte's "kind young servant," however, who discovered the growth under Topsy's lip. After a histological examination of a pathological specimen taken from an unusually compliant Topsy, Bonaparte's attachment to her "graceful toy" intensified as she feared the dog's "imminent death."

Bonaparte rendered the discovery of the lymphosarcoma in a short section entitled "The Sentence." The sentence or discovery condemned Topsy in Bonaparte's eyes to "the most atrocious of deaths."[58] In the following section "Poor Topsy!" the Princess repeats these words three times: "She looks at me with eyes overflowing with love." On the third occasion she adds, "and my own overflow with tears."[59] As she watched the tumor slowly spread to Topsy's right nostril, Bonaparte sought to master by repetition the progress of the cancer, to keep under a steady gaze, as it were, the love conveyed by Topsy's eyes. The repetition of the phrase becomes a means to restore Topsy to the status of a toy, to revert to the attitude she had toward the dog before the tumor was discovered. For a toy dog always exalts its owner. But this strategy of reiteration transformed into prosopopoeia. In "Implorations To The God Of The Rays," Bonaparte veils her position as benefactress of the Curie Institute in Paris and writes: "Somewhere in Paris there is a huge home where steel apparatus of a fiendish appearance glitters in the dim light of armour-plated rooms. They produce mysterious rays which sometimes heal poor human suffering from the most horrible of all diseases."[60] Bonaparte had, in fact, consulted G.V. Rigaud and his successor at the Institute Professor Lacassagne about Freud's cancer on several occasions.[61] Here, she asks herself: "Why have I not yet interceded for Topsy with the god who reigns over these realms?" Why did she not "disturb" Him? Topsy was, after all, "only a poor dog," and Bonaparte was sensitive to the possibility of having her request viewed as frivolous; she thus hesitated to intercede. Ultimately, she "dared" to "disturb" Him—not the doctors, but the god of radium.

As a child "Mimi" (Bonaparte) had numerous pets (a red squirrel, two marmosets, a mongrel bitch Diablette, a tiny dog named Zéphyr, and a fox terrier named Satellite).[62]

It was the loss of Satellite that dimmed the sun's brightness and the flowers for days, as Bonaparte recalls in the "Prologue." The writing of *Topsy* was not an occasion to dwell upon the loss of her childhood pets. Rather, in "Topsy Beneath The Rays," her dog's first visit to the so-called god of the rays awakened memories of her father: "Twelve years ago another body lay under the rays; my father, whom a similar affliction, though differently placed, was destroying. But I knew that the rays penetrated him in vain day after day."[63] In August 1922, Prince Roland underwent an operation on his prostate gland. At that time, Marie had left him "alone in his suffering" for a tryst with her lover.[64] It was not until almost a year later in April 1923 that Bonaparte learned the nature of her father's illness. From this moment forward she spent long periods at her father's bedside and thought of herself as a kind of guardian spirit in whose presence "nothing dire could happen." Prince Roland passed away on April 14, 1924.

Before Topsy's illness, the Princess had often left her for weeks and sometimes months on end, behaviour which she came to regret. She once again took up her position as a guardian of another loved one, but this time with the knowledge that the radium God might fail. Close to the time of her father's death, Bonaparte learned that Freud, whom she had not yet met, had undergone surgery for a malignant tumor in his oral cavity.[65]

As the facets of Bonaparte's identification with her ailing pet multiplied, she reflected more and more upon her own mortality. Together with Topsy in the garden of St. Cloud in the spring, Bonaparte evokes the blooming and buzzing confusion of life repeating itself seasonally in contrast to the inevitability of Topsy's death regardless of the effects of the treatment. "My hair is growing grey," Bonaparte notes, acknowledging that she too will perish in time, perhaps from an illness all too familiar to her. "Topsy And I In The Garden" is followed by "Topsy, My Terrestrial Sister," in which Bonaparte's "sisterly feeling" for Topsy is expressed by a list on which sameness triumphs over difference; that is, sisterly similarities bridge at various points the gulf between human and dog. The spell cast by the repetitive list is broken in "Childless Topsy" as Bonaparte regrets that Topsy, unlike herself, will never bear any children. But one soon learns that Topsy's presence assuages Bonaparte's longing for the companionship of her own children as she ages.

Throughout the summer and the autumn Bonaparte comments on Topsy's condition and promises herself that she will bring to Topsy a "merciful sleep" rather than allow her to suffer.[66] There are echoes here of Schur's agreement with Freud to end his suffering once it had turned irrevocably into torture. But Topsy understood nothing of this kind of agreement. Bonaparte again worries in "Lethal Lullaby" that her fantasies of Topsy's death may be seen as "too much," unwarranted, and even frivolous. Just when she had bridged many of the gaps between human and dog, new breaches appeared, exposing once again her initial awkwardness and hestitation in seeking treatment for a dog at the Curie Institute.

"Sepulchral Meditation" was translated by John Rodker, founder of Imago Publishing Company (London, 1938), Bonaparte's publisher and translator of her work *Edgar Allan Poe* (English translation, 1949). In this section Bonaparte does not attempt to bridge the gap between human and animal, but instead gives to the latter a decided advantage in matters pertaining to burial practices. For dogs suffer from none of the "burial manias" which afflict humans. On Topsy's behalf Bonaparte will arrange for her "that free burial to which I myself an not entitled."[67] This burial will not involve the "terrible customs" of the vault, sarcophagus, preparation of the corpse, etc. Unlike Bonaparte, Topsy will not be exiled even in death from the garden around which she roamed. Neither Topsy's burial nor Bonaparte's "Dreams Of Paradise" will be properly "Christian." Rather than angels and saints, Bonaparte fantasizes meeting her father, "young and healthy again," together with Topsy. The idea of this paradise served to unite Bonaparte's father and dog *beyond* the illness which normally linked them.

In the final sections of Part I, Bonaparte's writing is foregrounded in the text. She probes the incantatory effects of her writing of Topsy's illness as an autobiography and admits that, in the "Soft Hope Of Summer," Topsy "may be recovered in spite of my mournful poems."[68] Bonaparte adds: "And I think that up to now, it is only with ink and paper that she has been killed." Topsy may—her recovery is still uncertain or at least unbelievable—have defied Bonaparte's death fantasies and interrupted her premature mourning (a reaction to the fear of the imminent death of her dog in light of the death of Topsy's mother from cancer and the failure of Prince Roland's treatments). The Princess's poetical mourning ran ahead of itself, pulled forward by one side of a death fantasy (death from cancer) which jostled for position with the alternative of dying from old age.[69] *Topsy* rehearses Bonaparte's mourning for her dog. The pain she experienced did not arise from prolonging psychically a lost object, but resulted from the equally painful prospect of aging (complicated by her fear of dying, perhaps alone, from cancer).

Freud once playfully asked Bonaparte: "Does Topsy realize she is being translated?"[70] In "Before Leaving For The Summer Holidays," Bonaparte confronts her decision to leave Topsy for reasons of "work and health." "Duty" called her away—the duty of writing *Topsy*, with which she hoped to return. She is blunt: *Topsy* is "a book you [the dog] cannot read."[71] Bonaparte states forcefully and uncharacteristically that if Topsy were to die over the summer, "no one returns six hundred miles to watch a dog die."[72] As reality invaded Bonaparte's mourning, she was able to confess that, in "Autumn Home-coming," she "forgot her [Topsy] a little."[73] We do not find at the end of Part I of *Topsy* that reality-testing has facilitated the withdrawal of cathectic energy from her chow. Rather, reality-testing interrupts the poetics of mourning as the preliminary results of Topsy's treatment appear in a positive light and Bonaparte's own fear of aging and cancer momentarily diminishes.

At the end of Part I, Bonaparte noticed that Topsy's lip had begun to swell and feared a relapse, in spite of the positive terms in which the course of treatment were cast. The first section of Part II, "Topsy By The Sea," begins with the revelation that "the swelling in Topsy's lip has suddenly dissolved. It was an oedema caused by the rays."[74] Once again, Bonaparte travelled south for the winter, but this time in the company of Topsy. She is careful to qualify Topsy's recovery or cure with "probably," and only occasionally does her joy overwhelm her sense of caution in Part II of the text.

As Topsy's tumor shrank and the oedema dissolved, the chow regained her sense of smell. The text is full of references to inhalations, winds, aromas, smells of the seaside, breathing, and the scents of animals picked up by Topsy. The reopening of the dog's olfactory track opened a new chapter in her life story.

Bonaparte writes:

> You smell the washed up sea-weed. What does it say to your black nose? Surely it does not speak, as it does to my human eyes, of other shores beyond the waves that are, as here, caressed by the sea. But it speaks of a wider horizon, of other animals than those you know, terrestrial dog.[75]

This smell "speaks" metaphorically to Topsy's nose. It is coded linguistically as a sign of other animals (aquatic) and "educates" Topsy about them in their absence. This speech of smell also addresses human "eyes" and evokes another shore over the horizon. Bonaparte makes olfaction legibile and visible (written) and audible (spoken). She recodes olfaction through speech in order to try to capture its essence before it dissipates, but at the cost of importing a semiotic system which does not belong to dogs. Bonaparte continues: "Topsy, the greatest philosopher, strive as he may, will never know the visions which pass through your little golden head."[76] In spite of this linguistic recoding, olfaction cannot become a privileged means of knowledge, even in virtue of the dog's superior sense of smell and its semiotic "elevation" to speech. No matter how much this recoding enabled Bonaparte to "talk" further with her dog, no human can know the "visions" associated with Topsy's chemical sense. That is, humans do not know Topsy's "visions"—although the literature on the sympathetic understanding of the dreams of dogs and their "mental touches" may be traced at least as far as Lucretius[77]—because olfaction has never been aligned philosophically with representation, regardless of the extra complications of inter-species communication. What is represented here is the inability of olfaction in general to represent its object and, in particular, to be represented except by other signs made legible, visible, or audible. The "vain signs" which Bonaparte traces on paper while writing *Topsy* neither capture the wisdom, she ultimately admits in "Topsy And Shakespeare," nor the simplicity of a dog "who simply inhales the scented June air."[78]

Topsy comes to assume, however, Bonaparte's position as a guardian (the golden-haired lion-like chow resembled, in the first instance, a guardian lion of Egyptian mythology). Topsy guarded Bonaparte's beach house against intruders, just as Bonaparte herself believed that she protected her father and her dog against invasive tumors;[79] similarly, Topsy guarded Marie and Eugénie while they slept in the garden of St. Cloud on summer nights.[80] This theme is carried forward in the final section of the book, "Talisman Of Life." Bonaparte recalls that as a child her nurse Mimau (Marie-Claire Bernardini) comforted her when she was ill. Mimau assured little Mimi "that death would not enter" her like it had entered Princess Roland in the form of an embolism a month after a difficult pregnancy and childbirth.[81] With Mimau long since deceased (April 1919), her own children grown, and her husband occupied with his own interests, Bonaparte turned to Topsy for company and protection when she again fell ill: " . . . whether people come or go, Topsy stays with me."[82] Just like Mimau, then, Topsy guarded the Princess and "by her presence alone must bar the entrance of my room to a worse ill, and even to Death."[83] For Bonaparte, Topsy was a child who did not grow up and depart; the little lion remained with her physically and emotionally for much longer than her liaison with the man she called "the Lion," Rudolph Loewenstein.[84]

The childless child-dog attached herself to a zoomorphic conspecific, Bonaparte, whom she "nursed" back to health. Bonaparte's repeated references to Topsy's refusal of "the male" and her difficult relationships with other dogs suggests that the chow looked upon Bonaparte as her conspecific, perhaps not for the purpose of mating, but at least as a 'sister' or parent object.[85]

Just as Freud relieved temporarily his concern over the political situation in Vienna by turning to the manuscript of *Topsy*, Bonaparte found "Respite From Things Human," as she put it, in the unmixed, nonambivalent attitude of Topsy toward herself and other people. This was, of course, precisely what Freud had praised in dogs. Throughout the summer of 1936, fascism spread through Europe and North Africa with the advances of Hitler's and Mussolini's armies and the civil war in Spain. The electoral success of the Front Populaire in France under Léon Blum in June brought oppositional forces into the streets in what Bonaparte describes as a "Revolutionary June." For the Princess, the "French workers clamouring for bread and leisure," the "big red banners," and the revolutionary optimism of defeating fascism provided little solace. Voices were raised in hatred, she notes, against "those like you [Topsy] and me who have bread and leisure."[86] Bonaparte read this political climate through her relations with Topsy since their relationship, she felt, had been indirectly derided: "That is why, Topsy, one sometimes reads in the newspapers of these men that it is not right to love your fellows, the dogs. They turn the love—truly often too exclusive—of some society lady for her lap dog, to derision. They are indignant, they jeer at her."[87] Bonaparte certainly did not include herself among such misanthropic society ladies, nor did she think of Topsy as a lap dog, or a *chien de luxe* of any sort. Still, her caninophiliac tendencies made her an easy target.[88] Bonaparte's trepidation did not prevent her from publishing a short article entitled "Animaux amis" in *Paris Soir* later in the year.[89]

At the end of *Topsy*, Bonaparte is able to take credit for saving her pet. By writing this faith in herself, she works through the fear that her canine interests may be turned against her as evidence of frivolity and as examples of the idle pursuits of royalty in a time of international crisis. The qualification that Topsy has "probably recovered" is, however, still in evidence. This final sign of self-protection alerts us to what remains unresolvable in this dog story: Topsy's impossible task of barring death from Bonaparte's room.

In the summer and winter of 1938, the sporting tabloids and Sunday papers of London reported Freud's visits to his chow at the quarantine kennels. It is not surprising that Freud's concern was deemed newsworthy in a nation of animal fanciers. These inane reports do not give one a sense of the textual and extratextual caninophilia present in the history of psychoanalysis—they simplify Freud's love for his dog, and the man himself. Dog loving becomes in this context an affectation of the aged, a comfort for the European refugee.

Topsy is, then, not only the story of a golden-haired chow. It is a psychoanalytic tale. As one pulls the threads of the tale, the lives and works of Freud and Bonaparte unravel and the ligature of caninity which bound them together is laid bare.

Gary Genosko
Toronto, January 1993

Notes

1 Ernest Jones, *The Life and Work of Sigmund Freud,* Volume 3 (New York: Basic Books, 1957), p. 141.

2. Michael Molnar, *The Diary of Sigmund Freud, 1929–1939. A Record of the Final Decade* (New York: Charles Scribner's Sons, 1992), pp. 46–51 [Monday 11 November, 1929]. Page references are followed by the dates of Freud's diary entries upon which Molnar expands.

3. Ibid., p. 70; Tuesday 6 May, 1930.

4. Matie Molinaro, Corinne McLuhan, William Toye (eds.), *Letters of Marshall McLuhan* (Toronto: Oxford University Press, 1987), p. 34 [November 3, 1934]; p. 44 [December 6, 1934]; p. 46 [December 1934]; p. 62 [February 27, 1935]; John P. Roberts, Ghyslaine Guertin (eds.), *Glenn Gould: Selected Letters* (Toronto: Oxford University Press, 1992), p. 1 [c. 1940].

5. Molnar, p. 61 [Sunday 9 March, 1930]; pp. 69–70 [Tuesday 6 May, 1930].

6. Molnar, p. 206 [photograph of Anna with Wolf in 1931, including caption].

7. Jones, *Free Associations. Memoirs of a Psycho-Analyst* (New York: Basic Books, 1959), p. 181.

8. See Molnar, p. 260 [Friday 12 May, 1939]; Jones, *Free Associations*, pp. 40–1. As Mervyn Jones attests in his autobiography *Chances* (London: Verso, 1987, p. 5), "there have always been dogs in the Jones family."

9. Arnold Arluke and Boria Sax, "Understanding Nazi Animal Protection and the Holocaust," *Anthrozöos* V/1 (1992): 14.

10. Jones has commented that "like most Jews of his generation Freud had had little contact with animals" (*Life and Work*, Vol. 3, p. 141). This does not explain, of course, his attitude toward the animals he did encounter. The status of dogs in the culture of the shtetl, for example, did not colour Freud's attitude toward pets. Mark Zborowski and Elizabeth Herzog explain that "to the people of the shtetl the dog is not a pet, but a symbol of brute strength and unpredictability" (*Life Is With People: The Culture of the Shtetl*. New York: Schocken, 1952, p.344). The guard dogs of both peasants and noblemen would attack the shtetl boys. The dog, then, was a dangerous beast. Knowledge of this bestiary would have enabled— perhaps even required—one to decode the obvious cultural and political meaning of German shepherd dogs under National Socialism. Freud's emotional investment in his dogs overrode this cultural code in spite of Martha's best intentions. As Paul Roazen explains in *Freud And His Followers* (New York: New American Library, 1976, p. 499) "chows . . . upset his wife Martha. Probably her attitude reflected the traditional Jewish

distaste for the animals who patrolled the boundaries of the central european ghettos. She would be angry when Freud put down his food for them."

11. Jones, *Life and Work,* Vol. 3, p. 141.

12. Molnar, p. 214 [Thursday 14 January, 1937].

13. Molnar, pp. 106–7 [Monday 5 October, 1931]; p. 283, note concerning Martin Freud.

14. Molnar, p. 171 [Monday 7 May, 1934].

15. Barbara Guest, *Herself Defined: The Poet H.D. And Her World* (Garden City: Doubleday & Co., 1944), p. 213.

16. Ibid.

17. Celia Bertin, *Marie Bonaparte: A Life* (New Haven: Yale University Press, 1982), p. 179.

18. Ibid, p. 192.

19. See Lynn Whisnant Reiser, "Topsy—Living and Dying: A Footnote to History," *Psychoanalytic Quarterly* LVI/4 (1987): 671.

20. Peter Gay, *Freud: A Life For Our Time* (New York: W.W. Norton, 1988), p. 540.

21. Anna Freud, "Foreword to *Topsy* by Marie Bonaparte," *The Writings of Anna Freud,* Volume VIII (New York: International Universities Press, 1981), p. 360.

22. Hilda Doolittle, *Tribute to Freud* (New York: New Directions, 1956), p. 162.

23. Ibid., p. 98.

24. See Rachel Blau DuPlessis, *H.D. The Career of That Struggle* (Brighton: The Harvestor Press, 1986); and Susan Stanford, "Woman is Perfect: H.D.'s Debate with Freud," *Feminist Studies* 7/3 (1981): 417–30.

25. Janet Malcolm, *In The Freud Archives* (New York: Alfred A. Knopf, 1984), p. 114.

26. Ruth Mack Brunswick, "A Supplement to Freud's 'History of an Infantile Neurosis'," in *The Psychoanalytic Reader,* Volume 1. Ed. R. Fliess (New York: International Universities Press, 1948), p. 101.

27. Janice S. Robinson, *H.D. The Life and Work of an American Poet* (Boston: Houghton Mifflin, 1982), p. 278.

28. Freud, "Observations on Transference-Love (Further Recommendations On The Technique of Psycho-Analysis)." Trans. James Strachey (modified version of trans. by Joan Riviere). *Standard Edition* XII p. 169.; "Bemerkungen Über Die Übertragungsliebe," *Gesammelte Werke* X (London: Imago, 1946).

29. See Michael Grant, *Myths of the Greeks and Romans* (Cleveland: Meridien, 1962); Mark P. Morford and Robert J. Lenardo, *Classical Mythology.* Second Edition (New York: David McKay, 1977).

30. Freud, "Recommendations To Physicians Practising Psycho-Analysis." Trans. James Strachey (modified version of trans. by Joan Riviere). *Standard Edition* XII (London: Hogarth, 1958), p. 111; "Ratschläge Für Den Arzt Bei Der Psychoanalytischen Behandlung." *GW* 8 (London: Image, 1943).

31. Jennifer Stone mentions this point in her article, "A Psychoanalytic Bestiary: The Wolff Woman, The Leopard, and The Siren," *American Imago* 49/1 (1992): 141.

32. Molnar, p. 214 [Thursday 14 January, 1937].

33. Jones, *Life and Work*, Vol. 3, p. 212.

34. Molnar, p. 215 [Friday 15 January 1937].

35. Jones, *Life and Work*, Vol. 3, p. 212.

36. Ibid.

37. Quoted by Reiser, p. 669 [Freud-Bonaparte 6.12.1936]; also Molnar, p. 233 [Saturday 9 August 1938].

38. Molnar, p. 233 [Saturday 9 April 1938].

39. Jones, *Life and Work*, Vol. 3, p. 224.

40. Ibid.

41. Marie Bonaparte [Princess George of Greece and Denmark], *Topsy, Chow-chow au poil d'or* (Paris: Denoël, 1936); *Topsy der goldhaarige Chow von Marie Bonaparte* (Amsterdam: Allert D. Langer, 1939); *Topsy, The story of a golden-haired chow* (London: The Pushkin Press, 1940).

42. Anna Freud, "Foreword to *Topsy*," p. 359; The relationship between Freud and the Princess was less poetic in the eyes of Martin Freud. In his *Glory Reflected: Sigmund Freud—Man and Father* (London: Angus and Robertson, 1957), he writes that in return for guiding the Princess through psychoanalysis, his father became a "commonplace dog lover" under Bonparte's influence (p. 203). Freud and Bonaparte also shared an interest in antiquities equal in intensity to their love of chows. Chows "may not be everybody's cups of tea," Martin Freud added. *Topsy. Die Geschichte eines goldhaarigen Chow* was reprinted in 1981 by Fischer Verlag, Frankfurt am Main.

43. Reiser, p. 669ff.

44. See Jeanne Schinto (ed.), "Introduction" to *The Literary Dog: Great Contemporary Dog Stories*(New York: The Atlantic Monthly Press, 1990); on "petting" see Marc Shell, "The Family Pet," *Representations* 15 (1986):121–53; on literary fantasies of bestiality, see Laurie Adams Frost, "Pets and Lovers: The Human-Companion Animal Bond in Contemporary Literary Prose," *Journal of Popular Culture* 25/1 (1991): 39–53.

45. Freud, "Totem and Taboo." Trans. James Strachey. *SE* XIII (London: Hogarth, 1953).

46. Sandor Ferenczi, "A Little Chanticleer," in *First Contributions to Psycho-*

*Analysis.*Trans. Ernest Jones (New York: Brunner/Mazel, 1952).

47. Freud, "Analysis Of A Phobia In A Five-Year Old Boy." Trans. Alix and James Strachey. *SE* X (London: Hogarth, 1955).
48. Freud, "From The History Of An Infantile Neurosis." Trans. Alix and James Strachey. *SE* XVII (London: Hogarth, 1955), p.114.
49. Jones, *Life and Work*, Vol. 3, pp. 244–45; see also Max Schur, *Freud—Living and Dying* (New York: International Universities Press, 1972).
50. Jones, p. 231; Molnar, p. 306 [note to Tues 6 December, 1938].
51. Freud, "From The History," p. 32.
52. The interpretive move from wolves to dogs remained in the family of *Canidae*, thus reflecting the probable phylogenesis of *Canis familiaris* from *Canis lupus*, although the ontogenetic peculiarities of the case suggest that dogs must have been 'earlier' than wovles. The Freudian bestiarist considers it to be a category mistake to mix whales and polar bears ("From The History," p. 48), for instance. Since wolves and dogs are not confined to their own elements, they often meet, unlike polar bears and whales, Freud believed.
53. Muriel Gardiner (ed.), *The Wolf-Man and Sigmund Freud* (London: Hogarth, 1972), p. 12. Wolf hunts were part of rural Russian popular culture and aristocratic sport, in both the summer and winter. Although Freud recognized the obvious fact that wolves travel in packs, he ignored the unnumbered pack in the story of the tailor and the wolf because it was unnumbered; Freud resisted the wolfpack formation and preferred a numbered herd of goats. I develop these points in my article "Freud's Bestiary, How Does Psychoanalysis Treat Animals," *The Psychoanalytic Review* 80/4 (1993): 603–32.
54. Reiser, p. 684; Bertin, p. 195.
55. Reiser, p. 687.
56. Ibid., p. 685.
57. Bonaparte, *Topsy* (Transaction edition), p. 36.
58. Ibid., p. 43.
59. Ibid., p. 47.
60. Ibid., p. 51.
61. Bertin, pp. 182, 206.
62. Ibid., pp. 46, 56.
63. Bonaparte, *Topsy*, p. 55.
64. Bertin, pp. 135–38.
65. Ibid., p. 151.
66. Bonaparte, *Topsy*, p. 80.
67. Ibid., p. 96.
68. Ibid., p. 105.
69. Ibid., pp. 113–14.

70. Molnar, p. 233 [Saturday 9 April, 1938; Freud-Bonaparte 13.8.1937].
71. Bonaparte, *Topsy*, p. 109.
72. Ibid., p. 110.
73. Ibid., p. 117.
74. Ibid., p. 123.
75. Ibid.
76. Ibid.
77. See Boris Sidis, "An Experimental Study of Sleep. Chapter IX: Experiments on Dogs," *The Journal of Abnormal Psychology* III (1908–9): 69ff.
78. Bonaparte, *Topsy*, p. 151.
79. Ibid., p. 124.
80. Ibid., p. 147.
81. Bertin, pp. 25–6.
82. Bonaparte, *Topsy*, p. 164.
83. Ibid.
84. Bertin, p. 168.
85. See Thomas A. Sebeok, "'Animal' in Biological and Semiotic Perspective," in *Essays in Zoosemiotics*. Toronto Semiotic Circle Monograph Series, Number 5 (Toronto: Toronto Semiotic Circle, 1990), p. 124.
86. Bonaparte, *Topsy*, p. 159.
87. Ibid.
88. "Caninophilia" is a term used to describe elements of Freud's and Bonaparte's interest in dogs by Patrick J. Mahony, *On Defining Freud's Discourse* (New Haven: Yale University Press, 1989), pp. 62–3. Mahony has on more than one occasion pointed to the heptadic organization of several of Freud's major works (*The Interpretation Of Dreams, Beyond The Pleasure Principle, Jokes And Their Relation To The Unconscious, The Unconscious*), and parts of works (Part IV of *Totem And Taboo*), placing these alongside Freud's seven trips to Rome, a city with seven hills, etc; cf. Mahony's lengthy question during the roundtable discussion in Jacques Derrida, *The Ear Of The Other: Otobiography, Transference, Translation*. Ed. C. McDonald. Trans. Peggy Kamuf (Lincoln: University of Nebraska Press, 1985), pp. 61–2. Although Mahony does not mention it, an addition to this list may be found in the ratio of 1:7 of human to dog years. Freud seems to have taken this into account, but only in an approximate manner, when he wrote to Jones (24.2.1935) that Wolf was over 11 years old and therefore as old as himself. In 1935, Freud was 79 years old.
89. Bonaparte, "Animaux amis," *Paris Soir*. October 12, 1936.

PROLOGUE
IN DOGLAND

PROLOGUE
IN DOGLAND

In spite of the wish of my husband and daughter to have dogs, I refused to do so for over fifteen years.

As long as children are still small, I would say, close contact in a house with pets is unhealthy and dirty. In bygone days, as a grown child, then as a young girl, I myself had had a dog, a funny little smooth-haired fox-terrier, whom I loved so much, that when one spring day, in the South of France, he died, the brightness of the sun, of the flowers was dimmed for a few days.

Watching my growing children, I would think: Why thus squander my heart away? Have we not sorrows enough on earth, which come to us through human beings, from children, without creating others by adopting dogs? In spite of the regret of my husband and daughter, I banished the small companions from the house.

* * *

But at sixteen my daughter underwent a long illness, and courage then failed me to deny her that for which she was forever imploring. The first invader to enter our house was an old English sheep dog, with long fluffy grey hair, and later, two little white dogs.

My husband then declared that he also would, at last, have his dog, and so he acquired the fawny splendour of a chow-chow with black tongue and thick golden hair. In this way Tatoon, descendant of the dogs of North China, and of those that are said to be eaten in Canton, came to haunt the steps of our house like some flamboyant dragon from the Far East.

He was soon given a mate of his race, and chow-chow puppies, golden balls of hair, rolled about in charming frolics on the gravel of the garden.

In this way Teaupi, familiarly called Topsy, the female chow whose name these humble pages bear, was born and grew up in our house.

*   *   *

The big grey dog now lies buried, also one of the little white dogs, and Chiki too, the mother chow-chow. There now remain alone in our town house Tatoon grown old, and his daughter Topsy.

*   *   *

For over four years, as I passed the entrance in going in and out of the house, I would brush by the golden hair of the two canine lares. I liked them for their beauty, their hieratic calm, seated there like little lions, with paws nobly extended and half-closed eyes. But Topsy, the young female, was the more affectionate, and when my daughter once left for a long time, she became my own companion, and even in some small degree took the place of the absent one. I would take her, more and more often, from Paris, to the big garden where I was born, at St. Cloud, over there on the hill beyond the woods and the river. A kind of intimacy grew up between us. When I left on a journey, however, I felt she might be an encumbrance, and so without regret I would leave her for weeks, and sometimes for months.

*   *   *

But one winter morning, when I myself was ill, the kind young servant who combed and looked after her showed me a small growth under her right lip. Topsy was taken to the veterinary surgeon and operated on. And this time she was good, and remained motionless, she, who formerly, with the strong and fierce character of her race, had never allowed him to come near. The pathological specimen, preserved in a bottle of formalin, was given to me for a histological examination, for the surgeon had said that perhaps—only perhaps after all—a malignant growth was to be feared.

One of my friends, doctor and biologist, took charge of the sections. The definite histological answer would take some time to come. There, as I waited, in my woman's heart, more specially isolated that year than ever before, a passionate affection, all of a sudden, declared itself for Topsy, who, until now, had been but a graceful toy to me. May be because she was going to be taken away from me, because I felt, without wanting to believe it, that her life, Life itself, was threatened in her, that I started to love her so strangely and fiercely, and to dread her death, her possibly imminent death, as the greatest misfortune.

I

TOPSY IS ILL

THE SENTENCE

THE SENTENCE

Topsy's sentence has been pronounced: under her lip, which is again swelling, there is a lympho-sarcoma, a tumour that will develop, grow, spread elsewhere, ulcerate, suffocate her, and condemn her in but a few months to the most atrocious of deaths.

POOR TOPSY!

POOR TOPSY!

She looks at me with eyes overflowing with love. It was in this same town-garden that as a puppy, a small ball of golden hair, she gambolled about, biting her brothers and sisters, and her mother's teats.

She looks at me with eyes overflowing with love. What landscape memories of other scenes lie hidden behind those eyes? The snow of Switzerland in which she rolled about for a whole winter, that crisp snow that reminds dogs from North China of the cold ancestral air? Or else the dappled shade of that other garden of mine, the great garden of St. Cloud, that paradisiacal universe of dogs, where mice run under the ivy from tree to tree, mice that a single crunch turns into a tiny docile toy? There too, crossing the shade and the light of the underwood, a squirrel or cat will at times awake the archaic hunting instincts. Then, with lifted head, and barking, for hours the dog will stand at the foot of the tree in which its prey has sought for refuge.

She looks at me with eyes overflowing with love, and my own overflow with tears. For soon, no doubt, mice, squirrels and cats will be able to run about in peace. They can do so now! For I dare no longer take Topsy to St. Cloud. The tumour under her lip, which has grown and spread till now it is inside her right nostril, from day to day deforms and obstructs it ever more, so that now she cannot run down the paths or through the grass without sneezing and sneezing again and again like the sound of a death knell. Alas, poor little Topsy, shall we soon have to bury her under the soil of the garden she loved so much, there to sleep, wrapped and enfolded in the shroud of her golden coat?

47

IMPLORATIONS
TO THE GOD OF THE RAYS

IMPLORATIONS
TO THE GOD OF THE RAYS

Somewhere in Paris there is a huge house where steel apparatus of a fiendish appearance glitters in the dim light of armour-plated rooms. They produce mysterious rays which sometimes heal poor human suffering from the most horrible of all diseases. Why have I not yet interceded for Topsy with the god who reigns over these realms?

Had Topsy been human, I should have already been to him. But I hesitated to disturb him, in spite of his friendship towards me, for Topsy is only a poor dog.

Yet life, august life, also dwells in her humble body. Why this distinction, which even I seem to accept, between a dog and a human being? Topsy, if she can be healed, has as much right to life as I.

At last I dared take Topsy to the divinity of the Rays. He said one could try to cure her.

TOPSY BENEATH THE MAGICAL RAYS

TOPSY BENEATH THE
MAGICAL RAYS

Without a struggle, and only a few groans, she let them tie her on to the plank, her paws outstretched and her head muffled up in a hood like a tortured being. For a whole hour the thundering rays bombarded her head, while I walked up and down close by. Perhaps the tumour is radio-sensitive: we shall know in a week. Maybe the hardening in Topsy's nose will melt away and disappear.

But there is still the rest of her body! If the illness should break out again anywhere else, all my life I shall feel I was to blame, and that I should not have waited a single day in taking her to the god of the Rays.

* * *

While the kind young man who cares for Topsy calms her with his voice, I, alone in the small adjoining room, am haunted by memories. Twelve years ago another body also lay under the rays: my father, whom a similar affliction, though differently placed, was destroying. But then I knew that the rays penetrated him in vain day after day; the effect, I knew, would not be lasting; the same divinity reigning over them had warned me. In my thoughts, in my memories, I hear the cries of my father, day and night his heart-rending moans, as the inexorable disease worked deeper and deeper into his body. Morphia alone gave him a few hours' respite. Topsy, the little dog, happier than him whom I loved so much, will she be saved by the magic of the rays?

TOPSY SLEEPING

TOPSY AND I IN THE GARDEN

TOPSY AND I IN THE GARDEN

Every other day Topsy's golden head is placed beneath the rays, which maybe will save her. Meantime, since it is lovely May, I take her out with me into the big garden of St. Cloud.

Here we are alone under the verdant shade, while at my feet, one paw extended in the chow-like manner, or lying quite relaxed on her side, she sleeps. I look at her, and at the same time listen to the rustling of the leaves and the songs of the birds.

Sleeping Topsy, ignorant of death, listen! listen! We are not alone in the big garden: birds are singing, the nests are full of eggs or little heads pressed close together, insects are humming, ants are hurrying along the earth, plants are breathing, their green leaves sprouting in the May air, the grass in the meadow has grown, and is strewn with buttercups and daisies. It is all living, Topsy, like you, like me, and will go on living after us.

Whether Topsy's head alone conceals the mortiferous cells, and the rays have cured her, or whether further down, under her golden coat, the death dealing cells, borne by her bright red blood, have grafted themselves on her breathing lungs, what difference after all does it make? Dogs live ten, twelve, fifteen years, and Topsy is already five years old. Five years more or less, perhaps nine, and Topsy's body will be laid just the same, in the earth, beneath the grass.

And my fate is the same. Ten years more or ten years less! My hair is growing grey; many a time have I seen the coming of spring. . . . If then, Topsy, some illness similar to yours, or some other, to-morrow, or in ten years, should attack me, the garden in which I grew up, the garden in which you will sleep, but from which I shall then be exiled—for people—less fortunate than dogs—are forbidden to sleep under the soil of their homes, the garden with the big acacias, the large chestnut trees, forgetful of you and of me, will nevertheless blossom and re-blossom just the same.

Topsy, we are not alone in the big garden. The life that animates me, that still animates your golden body, is not the only one! There are birds, there are insects, there are flowers, and even, when you spare their tiny lives, there are mice under the ivy.

TOPSY, MY TERRESTRIAL
SISTER

TOPSY, MY TERRESTRIAL
SISTER

We live in the same house, Topsy, with its roof either blue or grey, according to the weather, or at night constellated with little lights. We see the same huge fiery lamp rise each morning; the same cold light increases and decreases at night as the month wanes or waxes . . . The same forests, with their halls of pillared trees and ceilings of verdure, the same meadows of this earth like carpets patterned with flowers and insects, are meant for your light paws as well as for my heavier feet. The same musicians, the birds of the sky, play to us.

What difference can it make to the sisterly feeling I bear you if to all this you feel otherwise than I? The air we breathe is the same in truth, penetrated by the same fragrance of gardens and woods, though you doubtless enjoy them physically more than I, your doggy sense of smell being more acute than my poor human one. Better than I, you savour the soft scent of the earth from which grass springs and daisies bloom, but I am compensated by my soul's understanding of the poetry that is spring and the march of the seasons.

Despite the gulf that separates our races, Topsy, you are still my sister, my terrestrial sister. A same red blood flows in your arteries and veins pulsating from a same heart; a same warm life intoxicates us of a morning when the sun calls us out. At our meals we share the same tasty flesh from the same victims, the same ground flour from the same corn gilded by the same sun, be it kneaded into bread or Italian paste; that same sugar which sweetens my tea, you crush with delight between your greedy teeth. Your light paws and my arms and legs are controlled by the same muscles. At nightfall, tired by our activities of the day, a similar weariness, mounting to our brain from our muscles, our blood, our nerves, forces us each to lay those weary muscles on a bed or low cushion, to close our eyes, and sink into the same blissful slumber. A same death, one evening of ultimate weariness, will lay us in the earth.

CHILDLESS TOPSY

CHILDLESS TOPSY

We still do not know whether Topsy will be cured or not. The swelling of her lip has subsided, but further down in her body, will the disease begin again?

Topsy, little spark of life, why, when miraculous life was yours, did you always, whenever the life-giving cells were stirring in your loins, obstinately squat down and bare your teeth, repelling the approaches of the male?

Now the illness is in you, and never again, should you be cured, shall I take your head and your loins in my arms, to try and persuade you to receive the male. Never will you know the happiness of small paws, of small greedy lips upon your teats, and when you lie down under the earth of the garden to sleep for ever, above you, amid the flowers and the grass, no little ones, born of you, will be playing.

I, Topsy, have given two scions to the human race. I have passed on the life I received; not you.

OUR ANCESTORS
AND OUR DESCENDANTS

OUR ANCESTORS
AND OUR DESCENDANTS

I know about many of my ancestors, but on two or three sides, beyond my grand-parents, do not know from whom I descend. On this subject, I know little more than Topsy.

Topsy, who were your remote forefathers? Further than any pedigree can go, on what day, on what ship, did white pirates carry away your black-tongued, golden-haired ancestors from the shores of China? And earlier still, what was the life of the ancestors of these migrating forefathers, red or fair chow-chows, and at the feet of which monks, in what Chinese monastery, did they sit?

They say that, in the monasteries over there, only the blue chow-chows are considered noble, and that the red are those of the poor, whose houses they guard, and that they eat them, as also the black, in Canton, for magical purposes. And did your ancestors hunt wolves, and did they draw sledges over the snow? I do not know.

All I know is that I love your golden hair, and that you became my constant companion as my children, grown up, went away more and more often. Life, tragic and normal, means that one's children grow remoter from one just when the parents are growing old. Parents, when young themselves, have their lives filled with other emotions besides love for their children, and no doubt the children often suffer in silence. But later, when our lives are ebbing away, our children seem to hit back at us; jealous life progressing draws them away from us. . . . Thus Time marks His passing.

*   *   *

And so, on certain days, Topsy seemed to pair off with me, and we made a kind of unique self absorbed couple, and the garden walls shut in our close happiness.

Far away, nations might clamour threateningly, money markets collapse, but you knew nothing of it all. The newspapers on the little table by my side, at the foot of the chestnut tree, told of this. If I read them but little, for you they were merely rubbish which you hardly noticed.

That is why your presence, in the sun-streaked shade of the garden, was so calm and so comforting to me. Dogs are ignorant of the extent and the bitterness of human quarrels, their quarrels being limited and short-lived. True, I was forced to lock up in the enclosure next door the beautiful chow-mongrel, your niece, whose coat, as golden as yours, envelops the slender figure of the Alsatian. For the moment you saw her, all your hair would jealously stand on end, and your teeth and furious voice begin to threaten. Good dogs are not always good. But Topsy, like the trees and the flowers around us, knew nothing of the complications of human quarrels, and only knew how to love me.

It is this humble communion of Topsy, the little dog, with me, the ageing woman, that nature, as with a lightning flash, came to disturb the day, the morning, when, under her right lip, I felt a little hardening.

MAGICAL DOG

MAGICAL DOG

We still do not know whether Topsy is cured.

I loved you before, Topsy, but not as I do now you are ill.

You have become, for me, a magical dog.

When you are laid down beneath the grassy incline which slopes away on the other side of the road, who will guard my door at night?

The shade of the big garden is full of hostile powers. There may be there, under the nocturnal trees, prowlers who have scaled the walls of the garden, thieves who will try to force the door of the house. Who will warn me, when you are gone?

The shade of the big garden at night is full of even more redoubtable powers: under the nocturnal trees seem to roam the ghosts of those that are gone—my mother, my dead mother, who wants her child back; my dead father come back to claim me. When you are gone, Topsy, who will guard me from these ghosts?

My life, like yours, Topsy, is declining, and when you will no longer be guarding the door of my room, it will be Death, the roaming Death that prowls in the garden, who will, perhaps, come into my house, into my room.

IN THE MEADOW

TOPSY'S HEART

TOPSY'S HEART

June has come, with days full of warmth.

In between each treatment which she undergoes every two or three days, I take Topsy back to St. Cloud in the evening.

Topsy, having slept the whole night in the passage, against my door, as soon as I wake I open the other door for her, the big glass one, the one downstairs which opens on to the garden steps, and immediately Topsy rushes off in circles over the grass. I shut the door behind her and go upstairs again to get ready to go out in the garden too. Then, very soon, from downstairs, small groans and yelpings can be heard. It is Topsy calling me, seated quite close to the glass door of the house.

For Topsy is not like her old father, the independent male, in his impenetrable forest of red hair. Topsy is not like her small companion, the playful little white fox-terrier, who is jumping about even now in the grass. For these two, the garden, with its coppices, its ivy, its wood-mice, its pathways, its small fields, is a joy in itself; for Topsy, the affectionate chow, the garden, in spite of all its sun, its coppices and its small fields, means nothing without me.

Topsy cries until I come. Answering her call, I soon come down the staircase, and, as soon as I see her from the top of the stairs, through the glass door, wisely sitting leaning against it, I see her eyes deepen and her tail wag. She knows I am going to open the door, that she will come in: she will jump up at me and will quickly go up to lie down on top of the staircase, to wait until I am ready. For Topsy prefers the inside of the house with me to all the fairyland of the big garden, even though it be a dog's paradise.

But, if I go out, taking with me my daily work to my shelter under the trees, Topsy, happier still, will follow me. There she will sit, proudly erect on her front paws, watching the depths of the coppice, while I write things, trace signs on paper that no dog can read, even though I may be writing about them. The world in which the thoughts of humans dwell is impenetrable to dogs. But the bond which joins my woman's heart to Topsy's doggy one is none the weaker for that. That is why I love to have her at my feet, in the house or in the garden, and why the garden, without me, is not enough for her.

If, some day, that ill which entered into her, and which seems for some time at least to have been charmed away by the magical rays, should break out here or there, under her golden coat, the only merciful action would be to put her to sleep for ever. Even were she able to live on some few months longer without too much pain, we, human beings who think, would, without a doubt, be too afraid of the illness that her poor lungs might cough up, to keep her in our rooms next to us. I would fear for myself, for my children, the disease whose origin is unknown, which never pardons. Then, if we did not wish to put Topsy at once to death, we should be forced to banish her far away, perhaps to the large garden of St. Cloud, alone with the little white fox-terrier, who loves the garden enough to live there always, out of doors, happy without us. But Topsy loves us too much not to perish of sorrow, as much as of her illness, in the great garden, without her daily ration of love, which no food can replace. It would be better, Topsy—if you understood I am sure you would agree—that upon awaking one morning, I should take you with me in the car, and, stroking your head, bring you to the place where, without pain, you would be given eternal sleep. You would then be carried, asleep, to the foot of our garden, on the other side of the road, to the incline that slopes down to the hawthorn and syringa bushes. If, in the morning, you could no longer get up, shaking off the earth that would cover you, to come and cry at my door, to beg for admittance into my house, at least you would never have known the sorrows of separation. And you would be sleeping after all not far away.

TOPSY'S EMACIATED BODY

TOPSY'S EMACIATED BODY

Will Topsy recover or not? In any case, her body is growing thinner and thinner.

Perhaps the rays have not saved her after all, and as I contemplate her, lying at my feet, her emaciated flanks heaving and breathing, oppressed by the summer air, I think sadly that next summer the garden may have lost its familiar genius.

Morning after morning, Topsy is taken to the Temple of the Rays, her thin body is fastened to the plank, her head muffled in the hood, the right side of her muzzle in the invisible cone; but, do what one will, and in spite of her patience and the power of the rays, under Topsy's right lip the little tumour seems obstinately persistent, and even ready to start afresh. Her lip is swelling again.

All that the rays have given Topsy, maybe, is one more summer in the garden.

Before the autumn leaves have started falling, Topsy may have gone to sleep on the slope over there, beyond the road, under the falling leaves.

* * *

No other dog will run with me, Topsy, in the garden next autumn or next spring. The spectre of death shall not pass before me again. No, not before my death, or that of the human beings I love! And, as a dog's life is so short, to have one, to love one, is, if one still is young enough, gratuitously to invite Death into one's house.

In this way Topsy, my pretty live toy, from a flippant joy, has suddenly become the tragic messenger of the most atrocious of deaths—the death my father suffered, and which I myself may possibly suffer some day. Death by cancer.

Run in the garden, poor thin little Topsy, as long as you still can run! Jump over the branches which the storm, the other evening, pulled off the trees and laid on the paths! The leaves on the fallen branches wither, you too will soon be faded!

LETHAL LULLABY

LETHAL LULLABY

If Topsy cannot recover, I shall choose for her the sweetest of deaths.

This haunts me: I imagine, I picture, with fearful intensity, the future day of her death.

* * *

Eat, Topsy, eat without distrust, the food that I myself have prepared for you to-day. Look: there is no bread in it to-day, only the liver and the meat that you love so much. You will not notice the inodorous white powder that I have mixed with it.

This is the powder, Topsy, which makes one sleep, dogs as well as people. Men and women, suffering from insomnia, take a pinch of it to pass the night, asleep, until dawn. Men and women, when they are sick of life, take more, to try to sleep, and sleep without waking.

That is the dose that I have given you, Topsy. For why should you wake? To feel the malignant tumour which your deceased mother, who also died of cancer, may have left you, grow from day to day under your lip? To be able to breathe no longer, your nostrils day by day more obstructed by the atrocious spongy mass? No longer to be able to eat, the greatest of all doggy joys? For your soft lip to ulcerate, and gradually dissolve into pus and stench? No more to be able to chase cats and rats, or, when the sun is shining, run about under the leaves of the woods?

That is why, Topsy, my last loving act towards you was to

prepare this meal, this sweet and treacherous meal, which will put you to sleep for ever.

Your eyes will soon grow heavy, your poor eyes that the rays have already bared of their lashes, and I, whom you have loved so much, will fade away in a mist. Maybe under your closed eyelids you will dream one moment longer. You will see, tawny huntress, the field-mice you chased through the woods. You may see the snow of the mountains in which you rolled as a puppy. Then, as your slumber deepens, you will dream no more, as you enter, your slowing heart still beating, into nothingness.

Then, when you are thus sound asleep, I shall pick you up myself in my arms, like a child, and burdened with this load of ultimate love, I shall carry you to the waiting car. For your sleeping form might haunt the house; your corpse I could not bear.

And the car, which so often brought you barking to the joy of the large garden, would roll towards the laboratory where you would exhale your last breath.

We should arrive, we should take you out of the car, we should carry you, more and more soundly sleeping, to the table. And the veterinary surgeon whom you loved so little—prophetic little dog—would come near you. You would no longer defend yourself against him, you would be sleeping so well!

Without even trying to bite him, you would let him insert into the vein of your leg, for the last time stretched out behind you in the chow-like manner, the needle of the full syringe. And the lethal liquid would rush into your vein.

I should stroke your head, though you would not be able to feel it, during the time—a few seconds?—needed to stop your already slowing heart. The man would then feel your chest and say "It is over".

Over! My strolls in the woods, with my beloved little dog. Finished, the long nights, with her vigilantly sleeping at my door. Finished the petting, finished the loving. I shall leave alone—no, with the kind-hearted young man, who too will be there, and who, like myself, will doubtless be crying.

People may say it is too much to cry for a poor dog. But I shall have loved her, my little Topsy, as one only can love something close, familiar, and part of one's everyday life. And that is why, when her paws have stiffened, and her body has grown cold, and has been opened by others, to see inside, the better to understand what it was that doomed her, I shall have them bring back to my garden that which was Topsy. So that her substance shall dissolve in the earth that is mine, and at least be re-born—alas, but an illusory immortality—in the flowers, the grass, the leaves, nourished by my native soil.

SEPULCHRAL MEDITATION

SEPULCHRAL MEDITATION

When you are dead, Topsy, I shall have you wrapped in a white sheet, and softly laid on a bed of fine sand, remote and deep in the clayey soil of my garden.

Then, if you cannot again know, in that eternal dark, when the sun shines, I, at least, may imagine that you hear, through the dark and the mould, my footfall, revisiting you. . . . That is why I do not wish, you being dead, that men shall shut you in some box or coffin. Too well do I know what chagrin you feel, whenever some screen, even my door's, divides you from me. . . .

Men, you see, have always, throughout the ages, had burial manias for themselves. Have they not sought to pursue, beyond this existence—that only which is real—a second and phantom existence, including the body also, even though it moulder away in darkness. Thus, they have built funerary cities with houses and rooms, yes, palaces and halls for kings. Amid the sand, the rocks of Egypt, pyramids have risen, hypogea been hollowed out of the rock, to shelter the mummies of the Pharaohs. Alas! They but perpetuate death, these proud sepultures, these caves, these painted mummy cases, these bands, these resins which immortalize not what lives but what is dead.

I shall have laid you deep, deep in the earth of my garden, on a bed of fine sand that only a few slight bricks hold together, that you may always sleep soft. You will sleep, as in the past, on your side, in your gold coat, and with fast shut eyes. But the infinite universe from which you emerged, will have taken you back. You might hear above you the patter of the rain, the rustle of the grass. The roots of the trees will twine about your body, and from your vanishing substance soon they will draw their luxuriant strength, in spring. For your body—I know, I must accept it—will disintegrate slowly: water, season after season pouring through, will carry away atom upon atom of your hair, your skin, your flesh, your heart, your bowels, and your brain. . . . But, if the thought pains me, if I think, at times, that it will be horrible for you, I am wrong! It is the old ineradicable disbelief in death, even to the death of the body: it is that disbelief, engenderer, throughout the world, of all the tombs in all the cemeteries, which moves me when I am hurt by this thought. . . . No! When your last breath is exhaled, every vestige of life will have abandoned you: no more will remain of Topsy, than that over which my thoughts mistakenly linger. . . . That is why, peacefully, I should think, on rainy or frosty winter nights, that you feel it not: that your body, dissolving thus, has at least submitted to the august law of Nature.

Thus, Topsy, for you, I shall achieve that free burial to which I myself am not entitled. Somewhere, very far from you, for me there will be a walled-up vault, and within, a double or triple sarcophagus of wood and of metal. And within, myself, with flesh set rigid, doubtless preserved by various poisons, that I may make the final journey that will bring me to this place. Such is the terrible custom imposed on poor dead humans.

You—so I live long enough—in dissolution will already wholly have merged into the earth of my garden. Only your bones, skeletally sincere, that unlike the hypocrite mummy, seek no denial of death, will rest upon that bed of sand, deep in the clay, which I myself have had made for you. Perhaps, some day, human hands, burrowing in the earth, will uncover your little bones. They will say, the men of those days, if the past at all interests them, that a pretty creature must have lived here. Or else, if lost to all finer feeling they will simply shovel your bones aside, mingled with earth.

Yet, in the deep shelter which I shall have had hollowed for you, it may be that nothing will ever disturb you again. The leaves, the grass, the humus of each year, will heap themselves ever higher upon you, separating you always a little more from the light, the bustle. Then, in the fine sand, your bones will for ever remain, in alignment, preserved in their skeletal order, till the sun's heat fades from the earth. . . . [1]

1. "Sepulchral Meditation" is translated by Mr. John Rodker.

DREAMS OF PARADISE

DREAMS OF PARADISE

I am dreaming of a paradise, somewhere, where those we have loved here would be waiting for us.

But the paradise of the Christians, too hard and jealously human, repels me. Amongst the angels and the saints on their clouds, I should be cold. Some other mythological paradise must be mine, whence neither flowers nor trees would be banished, nor the animals of the earth.

There, when it was my turn to go, my father, young and healthy again, would welcome me coming through the trees and the ferns that he loved. By his side, in the meadow, amid flowers and butterflies, Topsy would come bounding along—Topsy, the little dog—my little friend, whom on earth he did not know, but who would have joined him over there.

She would come, oh, so happily, gilded by the rays of an eternal sun, and, nose uplifted, eyes staring into mine as in the past, joyfully welcome me in the Beyond.

And my mother, not far away, my mother whom I never knew, my mother the musician, under a canopy of eternal foliage and amid eternal songs of birds, would smile upon her long lost child.

All the friends I have lost would be there, talking in the grass, and would smile at my approach. There to welcome me, too, would be all the animals I have loved on earth, those of the house, as well as the wild ones of the forests, the birds of the woods, and even the fish of the sea.

There, by some divine action, cruelty would be at an end, an eternal manna would nourish the living; from there Death would be banished.

*   *   *

It is easy to understand that the Paradises which for so long human beings have dreamed of have sometimes seemed real to them. For desire is creative.

But I, I know that I dream, close to my little friend Topsy, who may be perishing here below. I know that the flesh is everything in life, that when the flesh is dead, the spirit is extinguished, were it the spirit of the greatest of men, or that of Topsy, the little dog.

I know that when my Topsy is buried under the ground, her spirit will no longer be there, nor elsewhere, that in the black mould there will be only melting flesh, crumbling bones, and a repellent tangle of fur.

I know that all that will remain of Topsy, as, soon afterwards of myself, save the short recollections of those who have known us, will be nitrogen, and carbon, and water as well, which will mount up to the clouds, and that there will be nothing more.

SOFT HOPE OF SUMMER

SOFT HOPE OF SUMMER

Thus May and June have passed, swinging my heart, enamoured of Topsy, from despair to hope. And now, with these first days of July, the growth under Topsy's lip seems once more to be dissolving and disappearing.

Sitting by the meadow, I look at Topsy running happily in the grass—maybe recovered in spite of my mournful poems. And I think that up to now, it is only with ink and paper that she has been killed. Life, splendid and ephemeral, has taken her back into its sunshine, like the birds in the trees, or like me, this July.

Topsy, Topsy, Death will come! But, happier than I, you do not think of it. As in the past, forgetful of your ills and of their harsh treatment, you run, you bark at the birds, you lap the cool water of the basin; you awaken and want to go out early to run in the grass. You teach me a lesson, little ailing dog, perhaps already cured, who know better than humans that life is the present, and nothing but the moment that one lives.

AFTER MICE

BEFORE LEAVING FOR THE
SUMMER HOLIDAYS

BEFORE LEAVING FOR THE SUMMER HOLIDAYS

Forgive me, Topsy, if, without knowing yet whether you are really cured, I am going away and leaving you.

The summer is already declining, the sun sets earlier each evening. There is over there, Topsy, a place where earth suddenly ends, and where water for miles and miles extends—blue water that shines and sings. There, at all hours of the day, I dip in the warm surge, then, in the transparent shade of the pines that rise from the sand, I write and write.

In a few weeks, Topsy, I shall come back from over there with a tanned skin and a book you cannot read. But when I return, two months from now, at the beginning of the autumn, you will, doubtless, either be healed or doomed.

Forgive me, Topsy, for going away and leaving you. You must stay where you can be looked after, otherwise, I would take you with me. But, little dog, if you were a person—someone as near to me as you are—duty, duty, you know, would force me to stay! So, forgive me for leaving you.

I must go because of my work, of my health. Nevertheless, yesterday, I returned from far, Topsy, on purpose to spend these few days with you, these youthful mornings of garden and sun.

You are right to love me, in spite of my coming departure, to jump up on me when I come out of the house in the morning; for I love you more than I have loved most humans, with your simple heart, your sincere way of loving and hating, of not lying, your character transparent and frank like a ray of morning sun.

You are right to love me, in spite of my approaching depar-

ture. For even if I were not to find you on my return, I should
have given you, beloved little dog, yet one more summer. Other
masters, as soon as they knew the nature of the swelling under
your lip, would soon have condemned you to eternal sleep. You
would not have seen the grass growing on the lawns, in May, in
July; lying under the ground, you would already be decomposed
flesh and scattered bones. I respected your short dog's life. I
knew that one summer for you equalled seven summers for me,
and that if a god, one day, had to decide whether now to put me
to sleep, or to prolong my threatened life, this is what I would
have chosen. You did not have to choose; the alternative was
unknown to you; I chose for you; and so I gave you, Topsy, this
summer in the sun.

*   *   *

But if you are to die, Topsy, I shall not be there. No one
returns six hundred miles to watch a dog die—above all, as one
knows that a dog's life can now be extinguished by slumber, and
that they do not know, falling asleep, that on that day, for the
very first time, they will never awake again.

That is why it is now, when you are apparently cured, and so
alive, that I ask your forgiveness. Life is short for poor humans,
but still more so for poor dogs. When two creatures on this
earth, which time winds endlessly round the sun, have found
each other, have loved each other, even though they be of different species, why must other affections, other duties, and work
that a poor dog cannot understand, be strong enough to separate
them?

SUMMER WISDOM

SUMMER WISDOM

Before leaving, I took Topsy to the god of the Rays. In spite of five years without metastasis or recurrence being, for malignant tumors, the classical delay before confirming a recovery, he says he thinks she is cured. And the persistence of this little life has illumined my garden to-day, and beyond that, nature all round.

*　　*　　*

But, should Topsy not die, she will have to grow old. Then her grace, before her, will die. She will lose her teeth—those teeth that are all the more fragile for having been irradiated, and some day, her eyes may lose their sight. Her body in any case, grown heavy, will no longer be able to bound in the ivy, as though shot upwards by her slim strong legs. Should Topsy not die, she will have to grow old.

Then faced by the ruin of her youth, I may think, some evening, that it would have been better had she disappeared in the full gracefulness of her vigour. The sight of her decrepitude will recall to my mind the old saying and will make me wonder if Topsy's recovery were indeed a gift of the gods.

*　　*　　*

While I am writing, Topsy is lying by me in the grass, and she is far from philosophizing. She is tired after having run and jumped so much after the field-mice in the ivy. She is dreaming, maybe, under her half-closed eyes, of her evening meal.

Topsy, once more I listen to your teaching! The sky is blue, and the spreading perfume of the clematis embalms the air. Each of us is alive, Topsy, like those insects, look, flying in the sun, which, wiser than I, are not speculating on the alternative of death or of age! Yet, if the unavoidable alternative, because of you, moves me so deeply, that is because it is also my own. I too, Topsy, I, who seem to you an eternal goddess, must die or grow old. But, though I know it, I do not believe it, any more than you do, little dog. The beating of my heart seems to me, as to you, as though it must be eternal. And this evening, this summer evening, so fine, so blue, when I hope to keep you with me, I want to believe that you, that I, that the insects in the grass, that the trees in my orchard, will live for ever, and without growing old.

AUTUMN HOME-COMING

AUTUMN HOME-COMING

Topsy spent the summer in the garden, in the North, while at the seaside, in the South, far from her, I forgot her a little.

But when the cold returned, and I was back in town, I recaptured, with Topsy, both my love for her and my anxieties.

The illness, the tenacious illness, that spells death, seemed again to be swelling her golden lip. How then could I rejoice in her thicker, silkier coat, or the glance of her two sweet hazel eyes?

*   *   *

I took her again yesterday to the god of the Rays. If this swelling of her lip is a relapse, which he cannot yet affirm, the illness will this time be without remedy. Topsy's lip cannot be irradiated again. Such was the sentence passed by the god. "Among the humans that we tend", he said in his slow and steady voice, "at least fifty per cent never recover. These are condemned to a horrible end. To kill them would be an act of mercy. But one cannot. So—if I loved an animal as you love Topsy, I should leave her the benefit of being an animal. I would not torment her with cruel and useless treatments. I would let her enjoy the end of her life happily, and when she really began to suffer, I would administer euthanasia."

Topsy understood nothing of the sentence passed by the god, and looked at him in a friendly way, wagging her tail. And Topsy was right to trust in him, since the god desired she should live her life in happiness to the end. A few more runs in the woods, the gardens, where, with the dead leaves, autumn descends, a few more good meals, and sugar that crunches in the teeth; then one calm morning to sleep and sleep. . . .

II

TOPSY IS HEALED

TOPSY BY THE SEA

BESIDE THE SEA

TOPSY BY THE SEA

The swelling in Topsy's lip has suddenly dissolved. It was only an oedema caused by the rays. Topsy is probably cured.

Autumn is over, and now comes winter, and my Christmas flight to the sunny shores of the South. This time, I have taken Topsy with me.

* * *

She runs along by the sea, inhaling the wind and the storm. Topsy, Topsy, little healed dog, looking at you I am prouder to have almost magically prolonged your little life, than if I had written the Iliad.

You smell the washed up sea-weed. What does it say to your black nose? Surely it does not speak, as it does to my human eyes, of other shores beyond the waves that are, as here, caressed by the sea. But it speaks of a wider horizon, of other animals than those you know, terrestrial dog. Their aroma, yesterday unknown to you, teach you that elsewhere, in other surroundings, there are still other animals than those you chase there, behind the railings, other animals than the chickens, rabbits, or cats.

Topsy, the greatest philosopher, strive as he may, will never know the visions which pass through your little golden head.

* * *

At night, when outside the storm howls, and the rain from the sea whips the walls of the house, Topsy, lying on the tiles or the carpet, sleeps by me. In Paris and St. Cloud, she sleeps at the door of my room, but here, at the foot of my bed.

For the house, built on a level with the sand and the sea, has but one floor, and once thieves tried to break in. So Topsy is my guardian.

But she is still more! Topsy is my friend, my friend, who, in this different from my grown-up children, does not ask to leave me, to travel. This Christmas, my son is in the snow of the mountains, my daughter in the sun of the desert. Topsy lives and breathes in a radius ten yards around me, and cries to rejoin me as soon as I move a few steps away from her. Dogs are children that do not grow up, that do not depart.

*   *   *

What will Topsy have loved when death comes to take her away? What balance-sheet will death draw from her heart?

Topsy will not have loved little ones that depart, as her body obstinately rejected the life giving approaches of the male. Topsy will not have loved, as women do, some husband or lover, nor will she have wept for them.

But Topsy will have loved good meals that do not deceive, runs in the fields, on the beach, or in the snow when in winter there is any, and the chasing of cats.

But Topsy, rather than chasing cats, than runs in the fields and in snow, rather than good meals, will have loved to sleep unsuspiciously by the friend whom fate also chose for her.

For Topsy's heart, when in my room she sleeps at the foot of my bed, all the same watches a little, and knows that, not far off, also reclining, breathes that magical creature, her supreme providence.

Who can reign completely, and in a lasting way, over a heart in this world? Would you allow me to, Topsy, faithful Topsy?

TOPSY'S WHITENED HEAD

TOPSY'S WHITENED HEAD

TOPSY'S WHITENED HEAD

After the long winter, spring is back again. In my garden, in the North, the grass is turning green again, the grass where, here and there, cowslips and primroses are pushing through. The cherry-trees are white with blossom, on the boughs of the big trees, everywhere, the young leaves, like green butterflies, open their wings between the flying and singing birds.

When the sun, between two showers, darts its silver rays through the thin foliage of the branches, they fall on the wet brown earth or on the ivy that richly carpets the underwood. But, at my side, as I lie at the foot of a big tree-trunk, they also fall on the whitened head of Topsy.

For Topsy's golden fur, formerly only white under the tuft of her large flowing tail, has, through the strength of the rays that saved her, gone white on her head. And Topsy, with her deep brown eyes, now resembles some "marquise" with powdered hair.

Some think she is ugly like this. But I love Topsy's whitened hair which tells me, every time I look at her, that she is probably cured.

* * *

When, in days of yore, in the forests, man, still savage, hunted wild beasts and pursued his prey, sometimes the ancestors of the dogs must have come, once night had fallen, to look for the leavings of this prey. Their chops dripping with blood, they would regale themselves on the same flesh that, not far away, in some cave, the forefathers of man had devoured. Man, jealous of his prey, if he still caught sight of them at dawn, chased them away. Sometimes he pursued them; but, some day or other, he must have killed a mother by the side of her puppies and have taken them. Then, as they grew up, they learned to hunt with him, to share his cave and his meals.

Since then, oh Topsy, how many dogs have arisen, have run in the woods and the steppes, then have laid themselves down for ever to mingle their bones with our bones, in this same earth on which you are now stretched! And in how many places! For everywhere on this soil that bears us, where the sole of human feet has left its imprint, the imprint of dogs' paws has followed.

The races have varied, but even more than the races of man, the races of dogs: there have been Newfoundlands, bulldogs, greyhounds, alsatians and dachshunds, and, from the snows of China, the chow-chows, blue or red dogs, with thick hair and black tongues, like you, Topsy.

*   *   *

In the bargain concluded in those times between man and dog, the dog sometimes had to pay dearly. For the easier prey, for the daily meal, how many blows? And the death of the dog which did not matter, when the master was tired of it!

Your destiny was not the same, Topsy. You have won in the prehistoric market! More than your meal, your home, and the petting; you have won the primordial weal; it is life that you have won.

Cruel man is sometimes good, and though he invented arrows and guns, yet he discovered the rays that heal.

It is the signature of this benefaction which may be read on Topsy's whitened head.

*   *   *

Topsy's head has grown white, because last year, when the spring, as to-day, was beginning, Topsy was fastened eighteen times on to the plank, then, on her head wrapped up in a hood, bombarded by mysterious rays. Already one of her teeth, the sharpest on the left of the upper jaw, has the top broken off. But the cells which were madly multiplying under her right lip have dissolved, and her lip is now flat. No longer does she sneeze, as she did then, by fits and starts, in the beautiful spring. The illness has stopped, life has continued, and, almost a year later, Topsy runs again, happily, amongst the flowers and the growing grass, in the same garden.

TOPSY AND THE OTHER WORLDS

TOPSY AND THE OTHER
WORLDS

Thus, Topsy sees another spring, and runs among the daisies.

Do you know, Topsy, that I am back from a journey, a journey to a country far different from that in which we now are? Over there, there are plains which stretch out to infinity with corn, with flowers of all colours, and mountains covered with snow under an all-blue sky. But why go on? You don't understand me; to you, there is nothing I can describe. And even if you had come with me over there, Topsy, what would you have looked at? Neither the Atlas, nor the blue or pink convolvulus of the Moroccan "bled", nor even perhaps the Arab with his donkey at the side of the road; your eyes, your nose, your bark, would have been for the dogs and the cats alone.

Topsy is ignorant of geography; she does not know that on the other side of the walls of the garden of St. Cloud, and beyond the road that leads to it from our town house, there are many countries, many climates, infinitely varied: Asia, Africa, America, and not only the snowy mountain slopes or the narrow shores of the blue sea where I once took her with me.

*   *   *

Topsy runs in the fresh grass among the daisies. She woke up in the morning when I myself got up; she went out into the garden, and went to rummage busily in the ivy for field mice. Then came back to sit by my side in the depths of the wood, her front paws solidly planted in the earth, her ears erect, open to the song of the birds in the branches and the sounds in the distance.

But when noon struck, she ran from the bottom of the woods to the house near by, answering the call to her meal, her nice hot meal of meat and bread. In the afternoon the hunt for field mice was resumed, broken by long rests at my feet, until the evening bell called her to her second meal. Then, at last, when night had come, after a walk in the starlight or the moonlight with me, when Topsy, quite pale, slips through the high grass like an elf having assumed animal form, she went up to lie down, faithfully, as every evening, at my door.

The horizon of Topsy's days is confined to these narrow joys, like her narrow forehead between her brown eyes. Even when, in a month, Topsy's still youthful body will call for a mate, Topsy's horizon will not broaden.

For Topsy obstinately and tenaciously refuses the male and will have to die childless.

*   *   *

Topsy will never have known, like most women, the joys and tears of love. Stranger to our sufferings, our pleasures, Topsy runs among the daisies like some prairie elf, and it is just that indifference to all that makes the glowing core of our lives that I love. Near her, I find rest from human beings, so wearisome, so heavy; she soothes me like the trees, the flowers and the grass. And when I stroke the silver-streaked hair of her little golden head that she stretches up to my caress, I feel something of the freshness one experiences when one inhales the scent of a flower.

*   *   *

Topsy runs amid the daisies, ignorant of the Earth, ignorant of Love. She runs amid the daisies ignorant also of Death.

The pity I sometimes feel for her is absent this morning. I love this tiny life which deems itself eternal, since its running paws so cheerfully deny their inevitable stop, one day.

Topsy has forgotten that, last spring, just when the daisies in the morning sun, as to-day, silvered the grass, she ran in the meadows sneezing without respite. Topsy above all does not know, and did not know, the significance of that sneezing: the cancer under her lip and in her nose, which was going to kill her. A few painful hours tied on to a plank, with an unknown and terrible apparatus roaring above, these Topsy endured under constraint, but with confidence, because she was tied, and because she loved us, too. Then she forgot, and summer has passed, then autumn and winter, and now Topsy is probably cured, and will never know, in her new-born joy of living, that she touched, last spring, the frontiers of death.

For Topsy does not know that there is a country where she and I will go one day, whence no one returns, and that is darker than the darkest of nights. And I bless her for being thus, and for not knowing that which I, alas, do know.

TOPSY AMID THE DAISIES

RESPITE FROM THINGS
HUMAN

RESPITE FROM THINGS HUMAN

My friends could be jealous of you, Topsy! For, in spite of all their affection, they could not offer me what you so freely give: respite from things human. When you appear, you do not tell me your sorrows in detail; if you have hurt your paw, one cry and that is all.

And above all, there is nothing in you of those mixed attitudes which are human, in which one loves and hates at one and the same time. You either hate, as you hate cats, frankly, totally, without measure; or you love, as you love me, sadly waiting by the door the moment I leave, and bounding with joy when I return.

ANIMAL SIMPLICITY

ANIMAL SIMPLICITY

When I go out at night, in Paris, on to my terrace, to listen to the nightingale in the "Bois" nearby, I like, Topsy, to hear your little steps on the sand, close to me. I know, however, that neither the song of the bird nor the poetry of the moon touch your dog's heart; the terrace is for you but a hunting ground. Whereas I listen, entranced, eyes uplifted to the moon, drunk with the perfumes of the May night, to the song of the nightingale, you, your nose in the sand, obstinately snuffle after the traces of rats. And yet it is you whose company I most prefer. You don't talk, Topsy, nor do you trouble my contemplation by the recital of your woes, your quarrels. And, above all, you are yourself part of this nature which bears, rocks, nourishes, and kills, but which is not human! A fragment of life like the nightingale of the gardens and of the woods, you share with it in my heart the animal innocence. And I contemplate around us, Topsy, rising to the moon, the big motionless trees that surround the terrace. Only the vegetable simplicity of the big trees and the little flowers is more soothing than the nightingale or than yourself.

A SPRING NIGHT
IN THE GARDEN

SPRING HAPPINESS

A SPRING NIGHT
IN THE GARDEN

It is so hot this evening that my daughter and I have gone to St. Cloud to sleep in the garden. No wall opposes its density between ourselves and the sky. Breezes pass, fanning my face and closed eyes, breezes that smell of the grass wet with dew. And when I open my eyes a starlit penumbra dominates the dark masses of the trees around me.

Not far from me my grown daughter is sleeping. We are alone; one asleep, the other already dozing.

I think of her. What destiny awaits her in life? But the grass scents the air, the trees whisper, a bird sometimes wakes up in the undergrowth, with a little cry, then falls asleep again. And, in the grass, at our feet, Topsy is guarding us.

Substance of another lineage, like the bird, the worm or the insect asleep in the night of the wood, but more closely related to us, Topsy, like us, lives and breathes. But who will ever know the picture that the universe reflects in her animal gaze? What this calm night, for me an exalted poem, means to her?

*   *   *

Seated on your haunches, your fore paws proudly planted in the grass, your ears alert, you search the shade, Topsy, with your eyes. A dog barks in the distance: you raise your ears in that direction. A cat mews, and you scamper off into the wood. And you don't come back for a long time, hunting the fleeing prey between tree-trunks and bushes. The cat has taken refuge at the top of a tree and you bark and bark in the night.

Substance of another lineage than ours, Topsy, you doubtless come down from the wolves, which, in the woods, under the moon, howled as they pursued their prey. This night, in this peaceful garden in the surroundings of Paris, awakes in you the old atavistic instinct, whereas we women know, even out of doors, how to sleep at night.

*   *   *

I open my eyes towards the pale sky and gaze at a twinkling star. And I think then of the earth that supports my shoulders, whilst it is borne through space like a ship, laden with all the plants, all the animals of all the climates, travelling upon it like so many ephemeral passengers.

Topsy, now returned after her vain cat-hunt, is at peace, and lies down near us on the grass. Topsy knows nothing of all this. Her universe is the wood near by and the patch of grass on which she is now lying rolled up to sleep.

My own universe is vaster. I can picture the climates of the earth, and even know a little astronomy. But what is that in comparison with the infinite? Not much more than the wood near by, the patch of grass on which we three are sleeping and which, to-night, is the whole of Topsy's universe.

TOPSY AND SHAKESPEARE

TOPSY AND SHAKESPEARE

No more than the infinity of space can Topsy imagine that other vertiginous ocean: the infinity of time!

I sometimes think of it, and fear and tremble when I ponder that each minute of time is like a tiny wave of the big surge that will some day swallow me up.

That is why, desperately, like a shipwrecked person clutching at a spar, I long to cling to some achievement, even of small dimension, which would carry my name afloat to the future ages. In this way, our only too real carnal mortality seeks compensation in the imaginary immortality of a name.

* * *

Topsy, more shrewd, knows nothing of this illusion, and it is she who is right. Of what importance to-day to Caesar, to Shakespeare, are their names, their works even, since their brains have dissolved? And even if, in his work, a little of the creator's soul survives, at the end of the millennia accorded to the earth, this remainder of life would be also extinguished.

For who will read Homer or Shakespeare when there are no more human eyes? And even before, perhaps some other future men, of very different and unforeseen culture, will know them no more.

That is why Topsy, whose happiness is confined to the narrow limits of each day, is wiser than I, she who simply inhales the scented June air, whilst I strive laboriously to trace vain signs on this paper.

ON THE FRONTIERS
OF THE SPECIES

ON THE FRONTIERS
OF THE SPECIES

Topsy, should I die before you, my image, an uncertain phantom, will haunt you when you sleep. Now, when I am away travelling, sometimes, under your closed eyelids, you see the entrance door open, men come in carrying luggage, and amidst the luggage I appear. In the same way, if I were dead, sometimes in a dream you would think you saw me again. Then your sleeping paws-stretched out upon the floor would quiver, thinking they were jumping after my skirt, and I should not be altogether dead if, in the memory of some few creatures, of the humans who had known me, and in yours, my spectre would thus survive. But, whereas my grandchildren—should I have any—even though they never see me, should they be born when I have passed away, will at least know that I existed, will set a name to my portrait when shown my picture—if you had small ones, Topsy, they would for ever be ignorant of my existence.

The vain immortality of the human name stops at the frontiers of the species, and Topsy's little ones, of the dog that loved me so much, would to-morrow know no more than the birds of the woods, the fish of the sea, that I had existed. Should I leave my cupboards full of immortal writings—immortal for humans—for Topsy's little ones they would only be what they already are for the flies that dart through the room, for the flowers in that vase, and even for Topsy to-day: a worthless heap of the cellulose which men call paper.

REVOLUTIONARY JUNE

REVOLUTIONARY JUNE

Topsy, hark in the distance to the chant of the crowds. It is the French workmen clamouring for bread and leisure, which you, Topsy, get so easily. For there are poor humans, Topsy, who, when it is fine, as it is today, are not like you and me at this moment in a lovely garden full of leaves and grass, but who have to bang on sheet iron or rivet, in the metallic hell of a factory, hour after hour. Then they revolt, and sometimes go marching on the roads between the fields, or through the streets of the town, holding big red banners flowing in the wind, clamouring for leisure and bread, and also, Topsy, voicing their hatred of those like you and me who have bread and leisure.

That is why, Topsy, one sometimes reads in the newspapers of these men that it is not right to love your fellows, the dogs. They turn the love—truly often too exclusive—of some society lady for her lap dog, to derision. They are indignant, they jeer at her. But those, Topsy, who like your mistress, have large enough hearts to love you as well as humans, those who, like me, have brought up two children, paying in this way their tribute to the race, in the name of what should they be deprived, when they are growing old, of the sweet restfulness coming from your hazel eyes and your golden hair?

When I have stroked you, am I not more apt to take up my work again, that work every one owes, in his way, to his kind? You are for me my luxury and my leisure, after which the work, as with the workman, seems easier.

* * *

Listen, Topsy, to the singing of the men receding, as they glorify yonder their banner of blood. You don't know what these cries, these songs mean: you hardly prick up your ears. No more than when the swallows fly with loud cries, very far, very high above the trees and the rooftops.

You don't know, Topsy, what stretches beyond over the walls of this garden and the present moment. You don't know that men can make revolutions. You are no wiser in this than was the humble dog, last companion of the queen Marie-Antoinette. You are as ignorant of human tides as of the tides of the ocean. And the men who are marching, whose songs now fade into the distance, are to you just as foreign as the swallows flying to the zenith or the fish swimming at the bottom of the sea.

TALISMAN OF LIFE

TALISMAN OF LIFE

Topsy, when I am ill you stay at the foot of my bed. If it rains outside, or if the sun is shining, you stay near me, lying down.

Yet it is not exactly gratitude. You do not remember—actually you do not understand—what I did for you last year. You were ill, then, also, but differently, since in a week I shall be well again. You, Topsy, had under your golden lip that tumour which grows unrelentingly, until it suffocates the one afflicted by it, unless it be dissolved by magical rays. And it is I who, instead of allowing it to grow, or having you killed, as others would have done, took you to the rays which made it possible for you, Topsy, to see the spring this year, and now the summer.

I remember, when I was small, days of illness like these. I was no more ill than I am now, and yet I had to stay in bed. Then Mimau, my darling nurse, would not go out, and that alone was enough to reconcile me to my sickness. She stayed then, caressing me with loving hands and eyes, stroking me, giving me food and drink. And her presence alone told me—a child who feared death, the same death that had taken away my mother—her presence there in the room assured me that death would not enter. Mimau was there, my illness would be slight, just enough to permit this sweet and warm rest in bed with her close by, and a truce to tedious tasks.

Mimau has long been sleeping under the ground in the woods, in Versailles, close to my parents. But my attitude towards illness has remained the same as when she looked after me as a small child. I bless the slight sicknesses that interrupt the tiresome and daily duties. And I like the truce of the long restful hours, contained in the limits of the days as is my reclining body within the limits of the walls of this room.

Since Mimau is gone, who remains with me when I am ill, without going out? My grown-up children are both absent these days and will not be back for a week. My husband will, of course, come faithfully to sit by the table there, at the end of the room. But he has his occupations and will soon have to leave again. As for friends, they come and go, each having his own life. Yet, whether people come or go, Topsy stays with me, her muzzle stretched out on the floor, framed by her paws.

And as in bygone times from Mimau, a power seems to emanate from Topsy, as from a talisman of life. Topsy who, thanks to me, has probably recovered from a terrible ailment, Topsy, who has reconquered life, is for me a talisman that conjures away death. A simple dog, lying there by me, just like Mimau by the child that I was, she guards me, and by her presence alone must bar the entrance of my room to a worse ill, and even to Death.

March, 1935–June, 1936